DATE DUE

MR 19 '99			

DEMCO 38-296

Mountains of Fire

San Luis Obispo County's
Famous Nine Sisters
—A Chain of Ancient Volcanic Peaks

by
Sharon Lewis Dickerson

with
Photography by Joseph A. Dickerson
and
Graphic Illustrations by Marti Fast

EZ Nature Books
San Luis Obispo, California

with very special
for the idea and the help to
Virginia M. Crook—
Head Reference Librarian,
San Luis Obispo City/County Libraries

Acknowledgements

The research work on this book was made much easier because of the assistance of two gentlemen—**Mark Hall-Patton**, Director of the San Luis Obispo County Historical Museum and **Tom Esser**, educator and scientist. Each man has a very obvious love for his specific field of endeavor and each gave freely of his time, energy and knowledge in an effort to help me produce a text that is accurate and informative—while still being readable and enjoyable. Thanks to both of you!

I would also like to thank **John Ashbaugh**, Executive Director of the San Luis Obispo County Land Conservancy, and **Robert McDonald**, geologist, for sharing their knowledge and insights and for reading the manuscript.

Finally, special thanks must go to the reference staff at the **San Luis Obispo City/County Library**. Their knowledge, expertise and, most of all, their willingness to help, are much appreciated. And, they are to be commended on the fabulous resource tool they have put together in the form of the local history room.

Others who helped in many different ways include: **Marti Fast**, friend and business partner; **Sylvia Bender-Lamb**, Senior Librarian, California Division of Mines and Geology; **California Polytechnic State University Library**, Maps and Documents Section; **Joe Engbeck**, California State Parks and Recreation, Publications Department; **Alex and Phyllis Madonna**, Madonna Inn; **Emily Moser** and **Martha Thayer**, Reference Librarians, National Oceanic and Atmospheric Administration; **San Luis Obispo County Planning Department**, Research Department: **Skip Theberge**, Chief of the Ocean Mapping Section, National Oceanic and Atmospheric Administration; **United States Geological Survey**, Public Affairs and Publications Departments; **Yolanda Waddell**, Small Wilderness Area Preservation; and **Ed Zolkoski**, friend and publisher.

Preface

he view was very fine, finer than we shall have again soon.... To the southwest and west lay all the lovely plain of San Luis Obispo, the buttes rising through it—over twenty were visible—brown pyramids on the emerald plain.

—William Henry Brewer
April 23, 1861

San Luis Obispo County has many attractions—both natural and manmade. Sandy beaches and rugged seacliffs; oak-dotted hills and lush vineyards; Hearst Castle and Missions San Luis Obispo de Tolosa and San Miguel Arcángel are just a few. There's a natural wonder, though, that geologists consider to be unique in all of California—if not the world. And it's that wonder that Brewer—a Yale University scientist—referred to in his journal.

What Brewer called "the buttes" are the ancient peaks of volcanic origin that stretch in a continuous chain from the city of San Luis Obispo in the southeast to Morro Bay in the northwest, acting as a scenic divider between the Los Osos and Chorro Valleys. Like many visitors before and after him, Brewer recognized their geologic, historic and scenic uniqueness. (Note: Brewer passed through the county in the spring of 1861 while participating in an historic survey mandated by the

State legislature and conducted by State Geologist J.D. Whitney. The survey—which lasted from 1860 until 1873—contributed much to the understanding of California's geology and produced large volumes of material on geology, paleontology, botany, fossil plants and ornithology.)

Although there is some confusion over their origin and number, residents of San Luis Obispo County have embraced these peaks as their own—regardless of actual ownership—and refer to them collectively by a number of descriptive names, including the Seven (or Nine) Sisters, the Morros and the Cerros. To many, they are simply "our mountains." To geologists, they are the Morro Rock–Islay Hill Complex. (Note: Some historians and Spanish language scholars say that *moro* or *morro*—domed turban, knob or knoll—correctly refers only to Morro Rock, the only truly rounded peak in the chain. However, the *morros* is the appellation of preference in San Luis Obispo County as noted by the State Park Foundation's intention to name a proposed recreation area the *Morros State Park* and the San Luis Obispo County Planning Department's study entitled, *A Specific Plan for the Preservation of the Morros.* Accordingly, *morros* is the term which will be used throughout this text.)

According to the California Division of Mines and Geology, there are actually 14 peaks in the chain. Nine of these have names, recognized officially by the United States Department of the Interior's Geological Survey. These include—from south to north: Islay Hill, 775 feet; San Luis Mountain (or Cerro San Luis Obispo), 1,292 feet; Bishop Peak, 1,559 feet; Chumash Peak, 1,257 feet; Cerro Romualdo, 1,306 feet; Hollister Peak, 1,404 feet;

Cerro Cabrillo, 911 feet; Black Hill, 665 feet; and Morro Rock, 576 feet. Offshore, covered by 3,600 feet of water, there is a tenth named peak—the Davidson Seamount—a giant at 7,800 feet. (Note: Bishop Peak is often called Bishop's Peak. However, the Spanish called it *Cerro Obispo* which translates in the singular, not *Cerro de Obispo* which would make it possessive. Therefore, Bishop Peak is the name which will be used throughout this book.)

Interestingly, it took 422 years—from 1542 until 1964—for all of the major peaks to receive official names recognized by the Department of the Interior's Board of Geographic Names. Some of the minor members are still referred to by residents as "No-Name Hill." Others—the southeastern ones in particular—have local names which rarely appear on maps. These include Righetti Hill (aka Mine Hill), Orcutt Knob and Terrace Hill. And, according to local fishermen, there's another submerged peak—Church Rock—just west of Morro Rock.

The craggy facades of the nine major named peaks, though, are what have intrigued geologists, fascinated residents and visitors and inspired artists and poets since the beginning of human history. And it is these peaks—of similar origin, but individually unique—and the history, drama and folklore that surround them that are the major focus of the pages to come.

—Sharon Lewis Dickerson

Overleaf: The breathtaking view from the summit of San Luis Mountain encompasses the line of morros—often called the Nine Sisters—stretching from Bishop Peak to the sea.

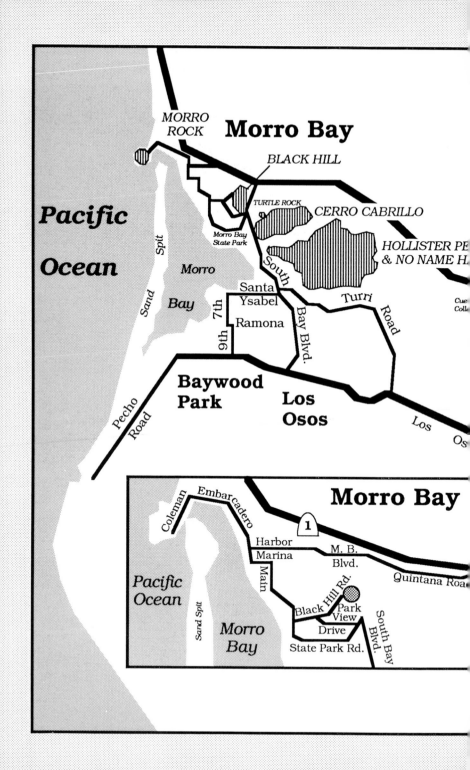

San Luis Obispo County's

Mountains of Fire

CERRO ROMUALDO

1

UNNAMED

CHUMASH PEAK

San Luis Obispo

101

amp Luis

BISHOP PEAK

Connor Way

Blvd.

Foothill

SAN LUIS MOUNTAIN

Valley

Road

Laguna Lake

Madonna

Road.

Monterey

Johnson

Ave

TERRACE HILL

ORCUTT KNOB

Orcutt Rd

MINE HILL (Righetti Hill)

Road

ISLAY HILL

Tank Farm

San Luis Obispo County Airport

UNNAMED

N

227

Contents

Section I

"...Some say the earth was feverish and did shake."

—Macbeth

Geologic Time Scale

Era	Years Ago	Period	Epoch	Features
Cenozoic Age of Mammals	10,000 / 2 million	Quaternary	Recent	Modern man
			Pleistocene	Ice ages
	10 million	Tertiary	Pliocene	Mountain uplift; cool climate
	25 million		**Miocene**	Grasses; grazing mammals
	40 million		Oligocene	Browsing mammals
	55 million		Eocene	Warm and subtropical
	65 million		Paleocene	Cool; age of mammals begins
Mesozoic	140 million	Cretaceous	Age of Reptiles	Last dinosaurs; flowering plants
	190 million	Jurassic		First birds; flying reptiles
	230 million	Triassic		First dinosaurs and mammals
Paleozoic	280 million	Permian		Early reptiles; pines
	310 million	Pennsylvanian	Age of Amphibians and Coal	First reptiles; coal; swamps
	345 million	Mississippian		Shallow seas; fern forests
	405 million	Devonian	Age of Fishes	First amphibians; age of fishes
	425 million	Silurian		Many shellfish; first land plants
	500 million	Ordovician		First vertebrates; seaweed
	570 million	Cambrian		Invertebrates
Pre-Cambrian	2.5 billion	Proterozoic		Bacteria; algae
	5 billion	Archeozoic		Earth's crust solidifies; first life forms

In the Beginning

eologists tell us that about 25 million years ago—give or take a million or two—much of western California, including San Luis Obispo County, was underwater. During this time of geologic history—technically called the early Miocene epoch of the Tertiary period (see geologic time chart on facing page)—narrow, shallow seas covered the Coast Ranges area from about Point Arena in the north to San Diego in the south and reached inland to engulf the San Joaquin Valley. Life in these seas—with minor differences due primarily to temperature changes—was very similar to coastal marine life today. There were clams, mussels, cockles, scallops, nautiloids, abalones, sea urchins, crabs and other shellfish—evidently in even greater number and variety than today. Bony fishes were plentiful as were giant (sixty to eighty feet long) sharks with six-inch teeth plus many species of toothed and baleen whales, seals and sea lions. Not all marine life was familiar, though. Along with the more recognizable ancient ancestors of present life, there was *Desmostylus*, a peculiar and now extinct beach-dwelling monster resembling sea cows and sea elephants.

The Miocene saw the rise of plains grasses (prior to this much of California was a subtropical region, warm, rainy and swampy) and mammals in all shapes and sizes prospered on the grass-covered plains and prairies. So rapid was the mammalian development during this period that the Miocene epoch is known as the Golden Age of Mammals. Among the land-dwellers who called California home were camels, rhinoceroses, New World pigs or peccaries, strange looking antelope with horns on their noses, small deer, saber-toothed cats, ancient dogs, huge land tortoises, the first long-toothed horses (an evolutionary step higher than the Oligocene three-toed horse, but still two steps lower than the modern horse of the Pleistocene), a variety of birds including hawks and ducks, rodents, snakes and lizards, lemurs and—perhaps the most exotic of all—mastodons.

It was into this strange and exciting world that the *morros* were born. Surprisingly, though, they did not erupt on the central coast landscape. Instead, it is believed they punctured the earth's surface much farther south at about the same latitude as Palm Springs. How did they get from San Bernardino County to San Luis Obispo County? The answer to that question lies in the theory of *plate tectonics* and is fundamental to the understanding of the origin of these geological wonders.

Underlying this theory—which was proposed in rudimentary form in the early 1900s, but not polished and accepted as standard until the early 1970s—is the fact that the earth's sea floor is constantly replenishing itself with hot rock that bubbles up from the subsurface at spreading ridges, vast underwater mountain ranges that extend through the North and South Atlantic, South Pacific and Indian Oceans. The sea floor—which can be compared to a giant conveyor belt—spreads slowly (up to ten inches per year) away from these

ridges in both directions, driven by convection
currents created by intense heat in the earth's
mantle. As it spreads, it cools, until, finally, it
sinks into deep ocean trenches at the edges of
continents and is forced back below the earth's
crust where it melts and either rises to the surface
as magma to fuel volcanoes or continues its jour-
ney back to the mantle to begin the spreading
process anew. The point at which the sea floor
dives beneath a continent is called a subduction
zone. In California's case, as the sea floor dove
beneath the North American continent, it scraped
part of its burden of mud and rock off at the continent's edge and, slowly—over a period of millions
of years—the sediment built up, forming the Coast
Ranges.

Basically, the theory of plate tectonics holds
that the earth's outer crust—the lithosphere—is
divided into six to nine major plates plus some
smaller ones. These plates—the Pacific and North
American being instrumental to the story of California and the *morros*—are from 30 to 90 miles
thick and float on the asthenosphere, a soft, hot,
semiviscous layer of the earth which, because of
the tremendous heat and pressure exerted by the
earth's mantle, flows plastically, allowing the plates
to inch their way around the globe at an average
speed of about two inches per year. The continents—permanent fixtures on the earth's crust
unlike the sea floor which is constantly subducted
and regenerated—are carried on the plates, but
bear little or no resemblance in shape or size to the
plates themselves. They simply float on the surface, carried along like logs stuck in an ice floe.
When, inevitably, continents carried on converging

plates collide, there is much bumping, crunching and crumbling and the plates become jammed, their movement halted temporarily.

Geologists believe that this is what happened about 20 to 25 million years ago along the coast of California. Apparently, when the Farallon plate (an ancient crustal plate separating the Pacific and North American plates) terminated subduction, the North American plate overrode the East Pacific Rise (the spreading ridge in the South Pacific Ocean which had been feeding sea floor eastward for millions of years). At this point, subduction ceased and the two massive plates—which were moving parallel to each other but in opposite direc-

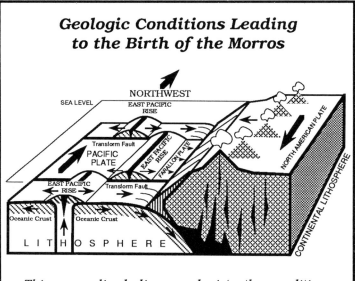

Geologic Conditions Leading to the Birth of the Morros

This generalized diagram depicts the conditions geologists believe existed along the California coast just prior to the birth of the morros. The arrows indicate the direction of sea floor spreading and global plate movement.

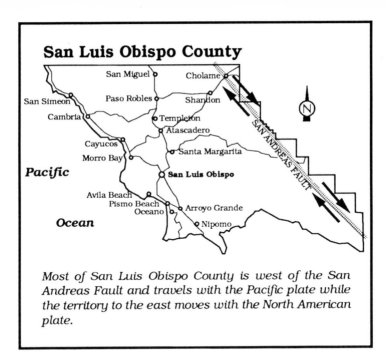

San Luis Obispo County

San Miguel
Cholame
San Simeon
Paso Robles
Shandon
Cambria
Templeton
Atascadero
Cayucos
Santa Margarita
Morro Bay

Pacific

San Luis Obispo

Avila Beach
Pismo Beach
Oceano
Arroyo Grande
Nipomo

Ocean

SAN ANDREAS FAULT

N

Most of San Luis Obispo County is west of the San Andreas Fault and travels with the Pacific plate while the territory to the east moves with the North American plate.

tions—jammed together, halting movement temporarily. When, eventually, the Pacific plate resumed its relentless movement northwestward, part of the North American plate broke off and went with it, creating a tremendous tear in the earth's surface. Since that time, that part of California west of the infamous rift—the San Andreas Fault—has been moving northwestward at a slow but steady speed, aided by earthquakes. (Note: Geologists call this chunk of California real estate the Salinian Block.)

Although the San Andreas Fault was the major break, there were many other faults that resulted from the collision. These breaks allowed hot magma bubbling up from the earth's mantle to break through the surface, forming volcanoes. It is suggested that the *morros* intruded the existing landscape at this time, the thick, heavy magma (about the consistency of toothpaste) erupting along a fault zone on the still submerged continental shelf to form a chain of volcanoes connected by a wall or dike in the subsurface. (Geologists have dated formation of the *morros* at varying ages. For example, Morro Rock has been dated at 22.1 million years, Black Hill and Hollister Peak at 26.4 million years (putting them in the Oligocene epoch) and Bishop Peak at 24.9 million years. However, they believe that the age variation is due to the dating process itself and that the *morros* are of the same age, having erupted simultaneously.) When, during the Pliocene, western California was upthrust and the seas subsided, the *morros* surfaced as active volcanoes, their cones several hundred feet higher than the erosion resistant dacite (a porphyritic igneous rock similar in composition to granite) plugs that remain today. (Note: Geologists remain uncertain as to how "active" the *morros* were. Whether they actually exploded is unknown. However, since there is volcanic ash nearby, some scientists speculate that the mountains did do a bit of spitting. Others doubt it. The vote, it seems, is still out.)

The intervening millions of years have been good to these mountains of fire. Through the centuries, their cones eroded away and wind and water sculpted the cooled magma into huge boulders which sit precariously on their sides and summits and dot the landscape at their feet. In the process, rock eroded into dust and piled up around their bases and in their nooks and crannies. Seed by seed grasses, yellow mustard, scrub oak and other native plants took root, softening the sharp edges and providing shelter for the many birds, deer, squirrels, rabbits and other wild creatures who call the mountains home. Seasonal creeks cascade

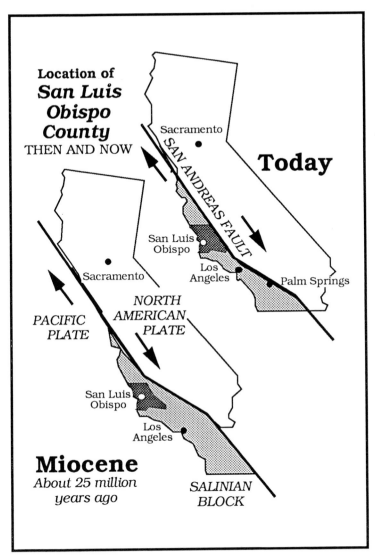

Location of
**San Luis
Obispo
County**
THEN AND NOW

Today

Sacramento

San Luis
Obispo

Los
Angeles

Palm Springs

SAN ANDREAS FAULT

PACIFIC
PLATE

Sacramento

*NORTH
AMERICAN
PLATE*

San Luis
Obispo

Los
Angeles

Miocene
*About 25 million
years ago*

*SALINIAN
BLOCK*

over the weathered rock and poppies, shooting
stars, buttercups, lilacs, monkey flowers and a
host of other wildflowers clothe the mountains in
springtime glory. Still, it is their craggy, weathered
facades—remnants of a world far different than our
own—that make these peaks the most distinctive
feature of the San Luis Obispo County landscape.

Composition of the Rock

As scenic features these buttes, stretching from Morro Bay to San Luis Obispo, are very interesting. They have no counterparts in the Coast Ranges. They are interesting to the student of petrography, also, as their rock characters are uncommon.

—H.W. Fairbanks, 1904

H.W. Fairbanks was the first geologist to seriously study the petrography of the *morros*. And, although his findings have been modified and updated over the years, his *Description of the San Luis Quadrangle*—written in 1904—remains a standard.

Fairbanks concluded that the *morros*—although a geographical unit—could be divided into two petrographically distinct groups. He classified the rock of Hollister Peak, Black Hill and Morro Rock as dacite-granophyre (*grano* meaning granitic, and *phyre* meaning rock containing distinct crystals embedded in a fine-grained mass) because it had a fine-granular groundmass "rich in potash, feldspar, and quartz..." Using Morro Rock as an example, he said, "The rock has a light-gray groundmass in which appear phenocrysts of soda-lime feldspar (oligoclase), biotite, quartz (rather sparingly disseminated), occasionally hornblende prisms, much decayed, and small pseudomorphs of calcite after some mineral, possible titanite."

Fairbanks classified the rock of the other *morros*—from Islay Hill north to Cerro Romualdo—as andesite-granophyre, saying it was "less siliceous and...properly classed among the andesites. ... The rock weathers yellow upon the surface, but the deeper portions are dark greenish gray to black. The rock is marked by phenocrysts of feldspar, biotite, and a ferromagnesian silicate. The microscope shows a calcic feldspar (labradorite), biotite, and enstatite, the latter being particularly decomposed, in a much altered fine-granular groundmass."

Today geologists classify the rock in all of the *morros*

as dacite (day´-site) or rhyodacite porphyry, noting that it has a fine-grained groundmass flecked with large crystals called phenocrysts. The principle mineral components include plagioclase (andesine-oligoclase), quartz, brown biotite, pyroxenes, green hornblendes and some potassic feldspar, chlorite, calcite, apatite and zircon. On the whole, the fresh rock is a dark gray to greenish-black, but exposed surfaces can weather to a yellowish-white color (Black Hill) or reddish-brown (Morro Rock). Modern scientific methods have corroborated Fairbanks' findings. That is, the rock which makes up the *morros* is 1) igneous—meaning it solidified from molten material; 2) intrusive—meaning it was emplaced in pre-existing rock; and 3) dacite porphyry—meaning it is similar to granite with a fine-grained groundmass dotted with larger crystals. Those of us who are not scientists refer to it simply as dacite and are perfectly correct.

Note: For a close look at rock quarried from the morros, *visit the First Presbyterian Church and County Historical Museum in San Luis Obispo (see pages 54-55) and Dutch's Fine Dining (see pages 68-69) in Morro Bay. Also, the statue* Pelican Family *at the top of the Centennial Stairway in Morro Bay was carved from a piece of Morro Rock.*

Volcanic Plug

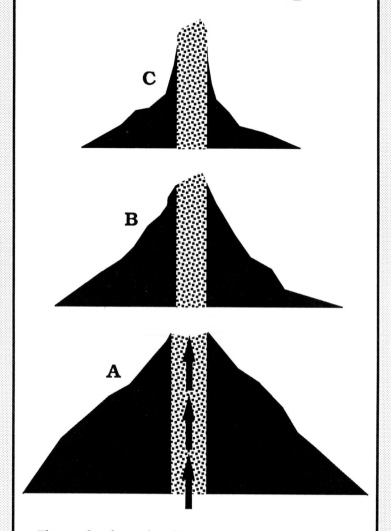

This stylized graphic illustrates the evolution of the morros. Basically, molten magma intruded existing rock, forming a volcano (A). Through the years, the magma cooled and plugged the volcano's vent. The soft outer slopes began to erode away (B), eventually leaving just the resistant dacite plug (C).

Section II

"We do not inherit the land from our ancestors—we borrow it from our children."

—Native American saying

Man and the Mountains

 *an Luis Obispo town lies in a beautiful, green, grassy valley...more like a plain, from four to six miles wide and fifteen or twenty long, running northwest to the ocean....*

Through this plain rise many sharp peaks or "buttes"—rocky, conical, very steep hills, from a few feet to two thousand feet, mostly of volcanic origin, directly or indirectly. These buttes are a peculiar feature, their sharp, rugged outlines standing so clear against the sky, their sides sloping from thirty to fifty degrees, often with an average *slope of forty to forty-five degrees! One near camp is beautifully rounded, about eight or nine hundred feet high, and perfectly green—scarcely a rock mars its beauty, yet the rock comes to the surface in many places. A string of these buttes, more than twenty in number, some almost as sharp as a steeple, extend in a line northwest to the sea, about twenty miles distant, one standing in the sea, the Morro Rock, rising like a pyramid from the waters.*

—William Henry Brewer

As noted in the Preface, William Henry Brewer—a professor of agriculture in the Sheffield Scientific School at Yale University—passed through San Luis Obispo County in April of 1861 while participating in a comprehensive survey of California's natural resources. From his writings, compiled in the book *Up and Down California in 1860-1864*, it becomes very obvious that this man of science had the soul of a poet and that both his scientific and spiritual selves were fascinated by San Luis Obispo County's mountains of fire.

It is not known for certain which of the "buttes" he and his small survey party camped by, but it is known that they were headquartered about two miles from "the curious old town" (San Luis Obispo). That fact—coupled with his description—suggests that the "beautifully rounded" peak was Islay Hill.

Islay Hill—beautifully rounded with barely a boulder in view—is likely to be the site of Brewer's camp in 1861.

During his stay in the county, Brewer climbed "a very rocky butte about four miles northwest of camp"—perhaps Bishop Peak. On another day he climbed a hill east of town. From its top he wrote, "The mountains to the north were covered with clouds at their summits, but their green sides, the great green plain to the south and west at our feet, ...the rugged buttes rising from this plain, the winding streams in it, all aided in making a lovely picture." Finally, before leaving the county, he hiked to the 2,900-foot summit of "the highest peak" in the Santa Lucia Range. It was from this vantage point that he penned the eloquent phrase that begins this book, calling the volcanic peaks that lay below him "brown pyramids on the emerald plain."

Brewer may have been the first person to write so profusely and poetically about the *morros*, but he was definitely not the first to recognize their uniqueness. Archaeological evidence indicates that Chumash Indians frequented the peaks as many as 9,000 years ago, camping at their bases and eating the roots and berries found growing there. Archaeologists speculate that the peaks may have had religious significance to these Native Americans who attributed magical powers to unique rock formations. Historians are certain, however, that the Chumash recognized Morro Rock as a navigational aid centuries before Cabrillo sailed into Estero Bay in 1542 and named the rock *El Morro*—a Spanish geographical term for a crown-shaped rock or hill. In fact, the Chumash word *lisamu*—shrine on the coast—is thought to describe this ancient sentinel which undoubtedly guided them in their canoe journeys up and down the coast.

In the centuries that followed Cabrillo's visit, numerous European explorers sailed past San Luis Obispo County, noting *El Morro* in their ship's logs. And, although there is no direct evidence, historians believe that explorers who ventured inland surely used the unique and prominent line of peaks as landmarks.

In 1772, when Father Junípero Serra founded Mission San Luis Obispo de Tolosa—fifth in the eventual chain of 21 and named in honor of St. Louis, Bishop of Toulouse, France—he located it near "a stream of the finest water"—San Luis Obispo Creek—and in the shadow of one of the *morros*. Later, the padres at the mission named this mountain *Cerro San Luis Obispo*—San Luis (Obispo) Mountain—and its neighbor *Cerro Obispo*—Bishop Peak. Both mountains—but especially San Luis Mountain—are very prominent in early drawings of the mission complex. And, as sketches and paintings gave way to photographs, these two *morros* continued to capture the eye of the artist. Today San Luis Mountain and Bishop Peak form a scenic backdrop for the city of San Luis Obispo which grew up around the mission and residents and visitors walking and driving in town still use these landmarks for orientation.

After Mexico's successful revolt against Spain in 1822 and the secularization of the missions which followed shortly thereafter, mission lands were divided into large ranchos and granted to Mexican citizens. At this time the *morros*—which had existed independent of ownership or constraints for eons—became "property" and figured prominently in rancho life.

Islay Hill became part of the 30,911-acre

Corral de Piedra and the Villavicencia family who worked the land built an adobe home in its shelter. That adobe—although worse for the wear—still stands and is the target of a preservation effort by the City of San Luis Obispo and several historical and cultural organizations (see pages 78-79). San Luis Mountain and Bishop and Chumash Peaks bordered the massive 32,430-acre Cañada de los Osos y Pecho y Islay and the smaller 4,157-acre La Laguna. Cerro Romualdo became part of the 117-acre Huerta de Romualdo—the only rancho granted to a Chumash Indian. Hollister Peak—called Cerro Alto prior to the 1880s—was within the confines of San Luisito and was named for the family who owned the land. Their adobe home still stands on the Cuesta College campus (see page 101). Finally, Cerro Cabrillo and Black Hill were connected with the 4,379-acre San Bernardo.

Eventually these large ranchos were subdivided into smaller ranches and the *morros* changed ownership. Today, all but Morro Rock, Black Hill, a portion of Cerro Cabrillo, Cerro Romualdo and the top of Bishop Peak are privately owned.

In her book *History of San Luis Obispo County*, published in 1917, Annie Morrison said, "The so-called 'chalk rock' (of Bishop Peak and San Luis Mountain) was used for building chimneys, fire-places, and dwellings in pioneer days. Boulders and stones, such as the millionaires delight to use in building their fire-places and walls, lie in heaps in fence corners or along streams." Historians agree that the *morros* provided building materials long before the "pioneer days" Morrison refers to. In fact, the original rubble walls of Mission San Luis Obispo de Tolosa contain boulders that evi-

This remnant of the original mission rubble wall stands in the garden of the San Luis Obispo County Historical Museum.

dently broke free naturally from San Luis Mountain and Bishop Peak.

By the 1890s, owners and developers recognized the *morros* as sources of commercial building materials and were no longer content to take what rock fell naturally from the weathering mountainsides. So, the blasting began. Morro Rock was the hardest hit. Between the early 1890s and 1963, one million, two hundred thousand tons of rock were blasted from its flanks, changing the shape of the monolith forever. Smaller quarries were operated on Cerro Romualdo and Bishop Peak. The former was opened in 1891 and provided rock for construction of the Southern Pacific Railroad while the latter was opened in 1897 and provided rock for the breakwater at Port Harford (now Port San

Luis) and for several buildings and numerous curbs and retaining walls in San Luis Obispo. In 1901, Harold W. Fairbanks of the United States Geological Survey said, "The buttes extending through the San Luis valley from town northwestward to Morro Bay furnish a most excellent and durable stone." His sentiments were echoed in 1906 when the California State Mining Bureau said of the *morros*, "These buttes afford very good quarry sites."

Eventually, most of the mountains were mined in one way or another—either by being blasted for rock or quarried for sand and gravel. Mine Hill—a minor member of the chain just north of Islay Hill—was mined for chromium during the 1890s.

Despite the quarrying activities which were marring the natural beauty of the *morros*, they

The Mazza House on Chorro Street in San Luis Obispo is constructed of Bishop Peak rock.

continued to be recognized as beautiful and unique. In its 1916 publication, *Guidebook of the Western United States, Part D—The Shasta Route and Coast Line*, the United States Geological Survey described the *morros* as the "most prominent topographic feature in the vicinity of San Luis Obispo..."

By the early 1970s, San Luis Obispo's quiet, green valleys—the plains Professor Brewer had found so appealing 100-plus years before—were beginning to fill with homes and motels and highways and there was growing public sentiment that the *morros* should be protected from development. During this time, the San Luis Obispo County Planning Department researched and wrote an extensive proposal entitled *A Specific Plan for the Preservation of the Morros*. Briefly, the Department—in an effort to act in accordance with the county's Open Space Plan—proposed that the *morros* be preserved under the Open Space Plan's "Scenic and Sensitive Land" subclassification, that is "land possessing outstanding scenic qualities worthy of preservation and land subject to undesireable physical changes if one or more elements of the environment is destroyed or altered." Unfortunately, the plan—which required full cooperation of the landowners—died, but the *morros* remained designated as "scenic restrictive"—the most protective of the open space classifications—in the County's Open Space Plan.

Although the formal plan to preserve the *morros* failed, those interested in preservation didn't give up. And, in 1975, when contractor-innkeeper Alex Madonna—who had purchased San Luis Mountain two years earlier—bulldozed a fire

road to the top of the mountain San Luis Obispeños hold most dear, the fight was on again. This
time, those who sought to preserve the *morros*
went to the State Parks Foundation—a private
agency that works directly with the State Parks
Commission, raising private money to fund state
park acquisitions.

The proposed Morros State Park (which did
not include San Luis Mountain) was to encompass
only the land above each peak's chaparral line and
was to be primarily visual—that is, save for a few
hiking trails, the land would be kept in its natural
state. This was not a unique idea. In 1928, Freder-
ick Law Olmsted, Jr., a nationally-recognized landscape designer, was hired by the newly-formed
State Park Commission to survey the State of California, noting areas that should be preserved as

*Turn-of-the-century workers building a retaining wall of Bishop
Peak rock in front of the Leitcher Adobe on Monterey Street.*
Courtesy San Luis Obispo County Historical Museum.

Many retaining walls built of Bishop Peak rock remain in San Luis Obispo today. This one on Chorro Street which had collapsed was rebuilt stone by stone in 1990.

state parks. According to his survey—published in 1929—he believed the *morros* were a unique geologic and scenic resource that merited preservation in the form of public ownership. However, according to William Penn Mott, Jr.—California State Park Director from 1967 until 1975 and former President of the California State Park Foundation—the state rejected Olmsted's suggestion because commissioners thought that the probability of development marring the *morros'* beauty was remote.

The Morros State Park proposal died like its predecessor—basically because it required full cooperation of the landowners and that was not present. However, the idea itself is still very much alive and continues to surface from time to time, spurred on by the efforts of San Luis Obispo County residents who remain passionately dedicated to the idea of preserving for tomorrow these unique landmarks that have been a part of so many of San Luis Obispo County's yesterdays.

Cerro Romualdo from Los Osos Valley Road

Section III

Of all of the *morros*, four—San Luis Mountain, Bishop Peak, Morro Rock and Davidson Seamount—have unique stories to tell that make them stand out from the crowd. These stories are related on the following pages under individual headings. However, the rest of the mountains have something to say also, and their bits of history and wisdom are detailed in the driving tour which begins on page 76.

"You will find something more in woods than in books. Trees and stones will teach you that which you can never learn from masters."

—St. Bernard

San Luis Mountain

*o say "our mountain" (when refer-
ring to San Luis Mountain) is a natural thing that's born in us.*

—Myron Graham
San Luis Obispo City Councilman, 1975

*San Luis Obispo Peak...and the rest of our peaks
belong to the citizens of San Luis Obispo County,
regardless of who owns them at the time...*

—Richard J. Kresja
San Luis Obispo County Supervisor, 1979

Of all the *morros*, San Luis Mountain is the
one county residents—especially San Luis Obispeños, those who live in the city of San Luis
Obispo—are most attached to. And, the attach-
ment—as illustrated by the two quotations above—
is most passionate indeed.

It's not difficult to understand. San Luis
Mountain—*Cerro San Luis Obispo*—was named by
the padres of Mission San Luis Obispo de Tolosa.
They built the mission—which was to become one
of the wealthiest in the chain of 21—in the shelter
of this ancient sentinel, using some of its volcanic
rock in the original rubble wall construction. Since
that time, San Luis Mountain has stood guard
while the mission evolved from a mean, primitive
structure built in a wilderness, to a beautifully preserved parish church, the pride of the special town

San Luis Mountain has stood guard over San Luis Obispo since the town's mission beginnings. Note in this c. 1887-1890 photograph that the mission (far right) sports a New England-style steeple and clapboard siding. Courtesy San Luis Obispo County Historical Museum.

which grew up around it. With a passion that burns fiercely in both "natives" and "transplants," San Luis Obispeños cherish their mission, their town and their mountain.

That passion surfaced in 1973 when Alex Madonna—local contractor-turned-innkeeper-turned-multimillionaire—bought the mountain which casts afternoon shadows on his famed Madonna Inn. San Luis Obispeños argued that their mountain—grass-covered and one of the least "volcanic" looking in the chain—should not be privately owned. If it had to be somebody's property, it should belong to the city or the county of San Luis Obispo and not someone like Madonna who made no secret of his plans to develop the mountain by building "something twice the size of the (Madonna) Inn" on its summit. (Note: Although Alex Madonna does own the majority of San Luis Mountain, he does not own it all. The City of San Luis

Obispo owns a 43-acre parcel on the east face of the mountain near, and including, the "M" on the summit. That letter, by the way, does not stand for "Madonna," but rather for "Mission High School" (today Mission College Preparatory School) built in 1925 and successor to the Academy of the Immaculate Heart begun in 1876.) Their pleas, although heard, went unheeded until the summer of 1975 when Madonna surprised city residents and officials by bulldozing a fire road which eventually encircled San Luis Mountain from bottom to top. Madonna said that the road building was prompted by a recent fire that burned brush on the mountain's summit and was simply a means to get at any future fires that threatened his property. It had nothing at all to do, he said, with his plans to develop the mountaintop. Much of the local citizenry, however, was not convinced.

Passions—which had been simmering—boiled over. Outraged citizens—who envisioned their mountain turning into another Matterhorn in a Disneyland-like setting—picketed the Madonna Inn. City officials expressed incredulity and threatened legal action, calling on the State Attorney General for help. Mayor Kenneth Schwartz was "at a loss to determine action. The road," he said, "is like humpty-dumpty pieces that are not going to be put back together. ... I'm quite amazed...because what has happened, has happened. It's a *fait accompli.*"

In an editorial dated July 28, 1975, George Brand, editor of the *San Luis Obispo County Telegram-Tribune,* wrote: "No issue in my (12-year) career as editor has so stirred the public and resulted in as many bundles of letters to the editor as has

The Academy of the Immaculate Heart (c. 1910). Courtesy San
Luis Obispo County Historical Museum.

*Mission College Preparatory School today. Note the "M" on San
Luis Mountain behind the school.*

San Luis Mountain as seen from the top of Bishop Peak.

the matter of Alex Madonna and his plans for San
Luis Mountain. ... Here by my typewriter I have
letters which because of space limitations we cannot publish in their entirety. Yet, the writers ex-
press themselves in a verve and zing which could
cause those who agree with them to chortle and
those who don't to curse." He continued with ex-
cerpts from the letters. Some were strongly in favor
of Alex Madonna himself: "I trust Alex Madonna to
preserve the beauty of his mountain for all of
us...." Others were strongly in favor of private
property rights: "...The matter should be closed,
since the owner is engaged in an apparently legal,
and in his mind, a correct use of his own land."
Still others were strongly in favor of the public's
right to protect scenic lands: "...Restaurants can
always be built, but mountains cannot be replaced.
Breaking the ground for the 'fire road' is the beginning of the end of our uniqueness and a stab at the

heart of San Luis Obispo." And, some were tongue-in-cheek: "I won't mind Mr. Madonna's fire roads so long as he posts pink lights along them." The reference, of course, was to Madonna's fondness for pink—a color which decorates everything from the napkins to the lamp posts at his inn to his construction company's fleet of trucks.

In the end, the city gave up its plan to purchase San Luis Mountain by using its powers of condemnation and eminent domain. And, officials dropped their lawsuits against Madonna when the District Attorney's office upheld a decision by the County Planning Department which declared that Madonna's actions were legal since "rural ranch roads are exempt from county grading permit procedures (and environmental reports)." But, the scar gouged by the bulldozers remains on the mountainside—and in the hearts of San Luis Obispeños.

Over the ensuing years, Madonna has continued to talk about his plans for the mountaintop which—according to reports in local, statewide and national news publications—include cutting the top of the mountain off to accommodate a multi-level restaurant-hotel-convention complex, built in Alpine fashion and surrounded by artificial snow. All of which Madonna believes would blend nicely into the hill and would be an asset to the community. And, there's the rub. Although many residents don't share Alex Madonna's views of what constitutes beauty—most, in fact, believe, as one resident put it, that San Luis Mountain "needs no further beautification"—they do not doubt the man's sincerity when he says that what he does he does well and he would not do anything that would be offensive to the people of San Luis Obispo.

Looking southeastward from San Luis Mountain. Islay Hill is prominent in the distance followed (south to north) by Mine Hill, Orcutt Knob and Terrace Hill.

Despite the attacks on his previous actions and future plans, Alex Madonna is gracious about sharing his mountain with San Luis Obispo County residents and visitors. It's a favorite spot with hikers and mountain bicyclists and, throughout the year he allows them access to the mountain via private rangeland, asking only that they respect his property by leaving fences intact so that his cattle don't stray. During the holiday season, he erects a large lighted display in the shape of a Christmas tree—his gift to the city—on the mountain's summit. And, at Easter, he hosts a sunrise service that is open to the public. It begins in the early morning darkness when hundreds of people gather near the Madonna Inn to start the hike to the summit. (Note: Madonna provides transportation for those unable to make the climb.) Once there, each person worships in his own way—some by attending the non-denominational service, others by marveling at the beauty of this ancient peak and the spectacular valley below. All enjoy the complimentary coffee and pastries provided by Alex Madonna and his wife, Phyllis.

In 1904, H.W. Fairbanks of the United States Geological Survey reported on the geology of San Luis Obispo County, noting in much detail "the line of buttes reaching from Morro Rock southeastward past the town of San Luis Obispo." He divided the peaks into two groups—those from Hollister Peak north and those from Cerro Romualdo south. Of the peaks to the south he said, "The most prominent and picturesque butte is known as Cerro San Luis Obispo." San Luis Obispeños would agree in part. But, they would take the comparison one step further. To them, their mountain is definitely the most spectacular in the chain.

The view from the summit of Terrace Hill includes the city of San Luis Obispo with San Luis Mountain (left) and Bishop Peak in the background.

Madonna
of the
Mountain

Alex Madonna would like you to think he's just another good ol' country boy. Which is fine, providing you know good ol' country boys who are multimillionaires....

—Michael Sieler
Los Angeles Times

Although San Luis Mountain had been a part of the San Luis Obispo County landscape for millions of years before Alex Madonna came on the scene, in recent years the destinies of the man and the mountain have become so intricately intertwined that it is difficult to separate one from the other.

Madonna—who purchased most of San Luis Mountain in 1973—spent his early years on the family ranch in the Chorro Valley where Camp San Luis Obispo now stands. When his father died in 1928, he and his sister moved with their mother to San Luis Obispo.

When Alex was 16, his mother bought an old Model T truck for $30 and used it to haul fill dirt for a backyard garden. When the job was done, young Alex convinced her to give him the truck, provided he bought the insurance.

While he was in high school, Madonna used his truck to haul sand and gravel, graded parking lots and driveways and generally did odd jobs. Eventually, he traded the Model T in on a newer truck and then accepted an old tractor from a customer in lieu of pay.

In 1938, Madonna got his first big break—and his first intimate look at San Luis Mountain—when Pacific Gas & Electric Company hired him to haul utility poles to the peak's summit. His old tractor couldn't make the grade, so he convinced a local hardware store to loan him a new tractor. It had no trouble pulling the grade but, when Madonna turned it around for the descent, it somersaulted, damaging the machine and the young entrepreneur.

Madonna finished the job for PG&E then went to the hardware store to face the music. Although the owners were willing to let him off a bit easier, Madonna felt obligated to buy the $4,000 machine. That was the end of his plans to attend college. But, don't feel too badly about his plight. In the years that followed, Madonna—who eventually bought the hardware store which sold him the tractor and the mountain which rolled it—built a multimillion dollar construction company that, in addition to building roads, dams, airports, canals and bridges in all parts of the state of California, has either built or resurfaced most of Highway 101 between Buellton and Salinas and worked on every inch of Highway 1 from San Luis Obispo to Carmel. But, Madonna didn't stop there. He also built the Madonna Inn—quite literally, boulder by boulder.

As the story goes, Madonna—who could not find an architect who understood what he wanted to create—designed the inn on the back of paper napkins. There were never any formal plans. He simply started building—and, with the help of his wife, decorating. The inn—which opened in 1958—is a mixture of architectural styles interpreted through the use of giant boulders and shocking pink paint. It has been called everything from "Early Awful" to "Holiday Inn goes Disneyland," but the fact remains that it is one of San Luis Obispo County's major tourist attractions, drawing over 1.5 million visitors annually. The rooms—all 109 of them—are highly individual and extravagant. Among others, there's the Jungle Rock and Bridal Falls rooms which have rock waterfall showers and the Daisy Mae Grotto which adjoins the Caveman chamber. The public rooms are no less flamboyant and include a coffee shop which serves quality meals on Blue Onion china—according to Madonna, the oldest china pattern in the world—a restaurant, a wine cellar, boutiques and more.

The Madonna empire isn't limited to construction and a world-renowned hotel. There are sawmills and timberlands and immense cattle operations to fill in the gaps. All in all, the story of Alex Madonna is the story of a boy who worked hard and made good. The story of San Luis Mountain—"our" mountain-turned-"his" mountain—is still unfolding.

Bishop Peak

he trail brings the traveler suddenly in sight of Bishop Peak... The town is fairly encircled with beautiful hills...the one just named being most conspicuous.

— John Muir, 1883

At 1,559 feet, Bishop Peak is the highest in the chain of *morros* and its rocky facade—composed of giant weathered boulders—makes it one of the most striking. So, it's understandable that John Muir—who was descending into the city of San Luis Obispo via Cuesta Pass—would make note of it in his travel diary.

According to historians, Bishop was named by the padres at Mission San Luis Obispo de Tolosa because the three sharp points on its summit reminded them of a bishop's miter or headdress. They called the mountain *Cerro Obispo*, a name which was eventually Anglicized.

Bishop was quarried extensively in the late 1800s and early 1900s. The first quarry—owned by Dr. G.B. Nichols of San Luis Obispo—opened in 1897 and, according to a *San Luis Obispo Semi-Weekly Breeze* account published on October 29 of that year, it was operated by the City Street Improvement Company of San Francisco. Rock from the quarry was used to build the breakwater at Port Harford (now Port San Luis). To facilitate the removal and transport of the huge blocks of rock

Bishop Peak as seen from the summit of San Luis Mountain.

that were required, the Pacific Coast Company—a narrow gauge railway company headquartered at the port—built a four-mile long spur track from its depot southwest of San Luis Obispo out to the quarry site. A report in the July 27, 1897 issue of the *Breeze* stated, "The new track will leave the main line of the Pacific Coast Railway at a point just 1000 feet below the trestle at the Odd Fellow's Cemetery...(now Sutcliffe Lawn Memorial Park on South Higuera Street near Madonna Road), thence following a fairly direct line to the base of the mountain...." The August 10 issue of the *Breeze* reported that work on the track was "being pushed rapidly ahead" and that, at the quarry, "a double hoisting and lowering track is being put in by...a San Francisco engineer. This track is to connect with the Pacific Coast line."

When the line was complete and the quarry operating at full speed, the *Breeze* reporter climbed the mountain to inspect the operation. His report reads, in part, "When the ascent of the steep mountainside had been made the newspaper man looked down upon a scene of beauty. Nestling to the left beyond San Luis Mountain lay our own fair city while to the right stretched forth the beautiful and fertile valley of Los Osos. Down the valley like a sheet of burnished silver the waters of La Laguna glinted (in) the light of day." After waxing eloquent, the reporter got down to the brass tacks of reporting on the operation and was especially intrigued with the double incline track that allowed workers, using a 20-horsepower locomotive and pulley system, to hoist empty railroad cars up to the quarry site and lower loaded cars to the spur track below.

The second quarry—located on the southeast corner of the mountain at about 1,000 feet—operated during the early 1900s. This quarry produced building stone used in foundations, curbs and walls throughout the city of San Luis Obispo. At least two of those walls—one on the corner of Santa Rosa and Palm Streets, the other on the corner of Chorro and Buchon Streets—were taken apart stone by stone, numbered, then rebuilt to conform with modern structural requirements. The quarry also provided the rock—described as "easily dressed" and taking a "good polish"—used to construct four buildings. Three of these still exist: the First Presbyterian Church on the corner of Marsh and Morro Streets, the Carnegie Library (now the San Luis Obispo County Historical Museum) on the corner of Broad and Monterey Streets and a private home at 1318 Chorro Street. The fourth

A spur track of the narrow gauge Pacific Coast Railway serviced the quarry at Bishop Peak. Photo c. 1905. Courtesy San Luis Obispo County Historical Museum.

Bishop Peak rock was transported to Port Harford (now Port San Luis) via narrow gauge railway then used to build the breakwater. Photo c. 1890. Courtesy San Luis Obispo County Historical Museum.

building, the San Luis Obispo Senior High School, was demolished to make way for a supermarket and parking lot.

The cut rock quarries on Bishop Peak were not worked after 1915 due, according to the California State Mining Bureau, to "the limited market for such material." However, rock was taken from the mountain as late as 1935 to be crushed and used as construction material. And, in 1979, Alex Madonna—part owner of the mountain—renewed activity at an open pit mine on the south side of the peak. The rock, he said, was to be used to repair roads on his ranch.

Along with its neighbor San Luis Mountain, Bishop Peak has become a special part of the city of San Luis Obispo. In 1976, the city had the chance to make it a permanent part by purchasing the peak when it came up for sale as part of a 450-acre ranch. One councilman who encouraged the purchase said, "I think there's a once in a lifetime chance to pick up the peak and protect it against onslaughts like those made to another peak." He referred, of course, to the fire road that Alex Madonna had bulldozed up San Luis Mountain a year earlier. But, the city eventually rejected the idea in favor of more pressing projects which needed financing.

Today, most of Bishop Peak remains privately owned. But, in 1980, owners deeded 104.31 acres at the summit to the California State Park Foundation. Although there were no stipulations regarding use in the deed, it was understood that this land should be preserved as open space for present and future generations to enjoy.

Bishop Peak is a favorite with hikers and

A hiker enjoys the view of rural San Luis Obispo from Bishop Peak's summit. San Luis Mountain is to the southeast (upper left).

rock climbers who reach the publicly-owned summit via "volunteer" trails which cross private property. Some San Luis Obispo County environmental groups hope to build a permanent trail along an easement provided by property owners. Until that time, most landowners are very gracious about allowing hikers to cross their land—which is posted with "No Trespassing" signs. However, they hope that people will respect private property. That means close all gates you open, do not damage fences, do not harrass animals, do not litter and do not smoke or build fires.

Despite man's eagerness to exploit it, Bishop Peak still stands tall and relatively unspoiled—a link between man's sketchy past and, hopefully, his more enlightened future.

High School — San Luis O[...]

San Luis Obispo High

Courtesy San Luis Obispo

School circa 1910-1915
ounty Historical Museum

The First Presbyterian Church c. 1925. Courtesy San Luis Obispo County Historical Museum.

The First Presbyterian Church today with rock nearly covered by shrubbery and vines.

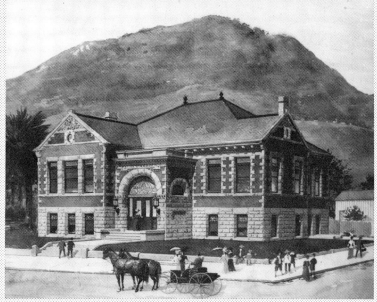

San Luis Mountain forms the backdrop in this architect's rendering of the Carnegie Library built in 1905 using some Bishop Peak stone. Courtesy San Luis Obispo County Historical Museum.

Today the building houses the San Luis Obispo County Historical Museum.

Within Easy Reach

Reprinted with the permission of Jeff Fairbanks, Managing Editor of the San Luis Obispo County Telegram-Tribune, *from the* San Luis Obispo Tribune, *Thursday, November 23, 1893*

"On the 14th day of November, 1893, and long before daylight, attired in a canvas hunting suit, strong walking shoes and with a stout staff in my hand, I sallied forth from the Cosmopolitan hotel intent upon reaching the summit of "Obispo," and from that point of vantage watching "Old Sol" make his appearance. The trail up the side of the rugged old "bishop," who has for so many centuries stood guard with his neighbor, San Luis, like a sentinel at the gate of an ancient city, is an arduous one to travel over, and they who would gain the summit must be prepared to endure fatigue of no light order, but as there is "no royal road to learning," so few pleasures of value are obtainable without adequate compensation being given. Reader mine, did you ever recline upon a hillside and watch the on-coming glows of a sunrise in a region of country where all the surroundings tended to the enchantment of their gorgeous splendor? If not then make use of your first opportunity to do so, for nature offers no grander or more enobling (sic) sight.

My destination was reached just as the first pink flush was tinging the eastern sky. Higher, higher it reached, broader and broader it glows, and clearer and brighter becomes the color which heralds the approach of the monarch of our universe. When the first curve of that majestic forehead comes into view above the horizon, how speedily the glowing body follows it. It seems at once to leap up into the full view of the watcher of its magnificence, and then how startling and grand are the changes over the whole wide stretch of landscape which lies before you. Hill, valley, mountain and plain seem to rock and sway as the light mist of night, which hung over and enshrouded them like a veil, is lifted and shaken and tossed about, until it is rolled up and tucked away in the gorges and ravines to be hauled forth again in the evening. There is a play of light and shadow at hide and seek with each other everywhere around, about, below and above you, the birds twitter, insects hum, and from a thousand throats in as many barnyards there comes the cheer of chanticleer's tribute to early rising, echoed and repeated until the sound fades away into the silence of distance. There floats a difference of airy fragrance about you, then that which existed but a moment ago, the flowers open their petals and wink their dewy eyes, the very rocks seem to rise up as if from sleep. Away in the distance, thirteen miles or more from Obispo, the limitless waters of the Pacific Ocean sparkle and glitter with renewed beauty, the whole earth rejoices at the nativity of a new day. Ninety-five millions of miles away, rolls onward the mighty traveller (sic) who has accomplished all this, a panorama so grand, so changeful, so inspiring, that the ablest pencil ever pushed along paper would be powerless to describe, or the most dexterous wielder of the brush to transfer a little of its beauties to canvas. This is sunrise seen from Obispo, an ample recompense for the labors of the climb. One more look around upon the landscape and I laid my hand upon my now complaining stomach, and fled down the trail making much better time than was done in the ascent. Neither, when I again entered the Cosmopolitan did I stand upon the order or disorder of my appearance, but seated myself as quickly as possible at one of the well supplied tables in the dining room where I made a breakfast which— but no, no man shall ever know what or how much I consumed at that meal. Suffice it to state that after a soothing pipe of tobacco there came over me a desire to tell the *Tribune* what I thought of sunrise as seen from Obispo's summit, and what a great thing it would be if there was a little Swiss chalet up there under the shadow of his Eminence's hat where a party might spend the night in smoking, swapping lies and similar divertisements (sic) until this unequaled morning dawning came." —H.G.S.

Morro Rock

outh of the town of San Luis Obispo there begins a line of peaks and ridges which extends northwestward for about 16 miles. It terminates in Morro Rock, lying in the ocean off Morro Bay. These elevations form the northern boundary of Los Osos and a part of San Luis valleys, and are separated from the Santa Lucia Range by the lesser valleys and rolling hills. This series of buttes constitutes the most striking topographic feature of the quadrangle. There are about 12, and they range in altitude from 400 to 1600 feet. Many of them are almost completely isolated and rise from the open valleys with bold and frequently precipitous rocky faces. Morro Rock, the most northerly of these buttes, rises from the ocean as a bare rounded mass of rock nearly 600 feet high, forming the most striking scenic feature of the coast of California....

—H.W. Fairbanks, 1904

Standing knee deep in the Pacific Ocean, Morro Rock—the northernmost member of the volcanic chain—is, without doubt, the most recognized, celebrated and photographed of the *morros*. It was named *El Morro*—crown-shaped rock or hill—by Portuguese explorer Juan Rodríguez Cabrillo who sailed into Estero Bay in 1542. But, according to archaeologists and historians, it is evident from remnants of Indian culture unearthed near the Rock that the Chumash most probably

Morro Rock (c. 1890-1905) was an island until 1936. Couresy San Luis Obispo County Historical Museum.

used the peak as a vantage point and navigational landmark centuries before Cabrillo "discovered" it.

Following Cabrillo's sighting, many other European explorers—including Pedro de Unamuno, Sebastian Rodríguez Cermeño and Sebastian Vizcaíno—noted the ancient landfall in their ship's logs. Then, in 1769, Captain Don Gaspar de Portolá—appointed governor of Lower and Upper California in 1767—led the first land expedition up the coast from San Diego to Monterey. On September 8, he and his men camped in the Los Osos Valley and Father Juan Crespí—expedition diarist—made note of the Rock in his journal: "To the south an estuary of immense size enters this valley, so large that it looked like a harbor to us; its mouth opens to the southwest and we noticed that it is covered with reefs which cause a furious surf. At a short distance from it, to the north, we saw a great rock in the form of a *morro*, which at high tide is isolated and separated from the coast by little less than a gunshot." (Note: Morro Rock has not always waded in the Pacific Ocean. During the ice ages of the Pleistocene epoch so much water was taken up in glaciers that sea level dropped several hundred feet, leaving Morro Rock high and dry—even during the very highest tides. When the glaciers and ice caps receded, the sea level rose and again surrounded the Rock on all sides. It remained an island until 1936 when the Works Progress Administration built the causeway—using stone from the rock itself—which today provides access to the Rock from shore.)

Since the beginning of human history, Morro Rock had been valued for its navigational and scenic value. But, in the late 1800s, it also became valued for the building materials it could provide. The blasting began about 1891 when rock was needed for the Port Harford (now Port San Luis) breakwater near Avila Beach. The 1896 edition of the California State Mining Bureau's *Thirteenth Report of the State Mineralogist* says of the Morro Rock Quarry: "It is near the base of Morro Rock, a conical-shaped peak at the entrance of Morro Bay, and is about 600' altitude. The rock is a hard, light gray porphyry, in which the feldspar is slightly decomposed. It breaks regularly, and good dimension stone may be easily obtained. It is quarried by contract, and loaded from the quarry on barges by a steam-power derrick. The principal part of the rock quarried is used in constructing a breakwater at Port Harford, and a limited quantity for buildings. The quarry is on a Government reservation."

In 1904, H.W. Fairbanks, a United States Geological Survey scientist studying the San Luis Obispo area, acknowledged the Morro Rock Quarry, noting that it furnished "excellent and durable stone for building purposes." Fairbanks,

An Ode to Morro Rock

Standing on the gentle sloping land,
    That rises back from Morro's shining bay,
I look along the shining stretch of strand,
    And hear the roar of surf, and see the spray
That rises white and pure as mountain snow,
    With showers of diamond drops flung far and wide.

Flashing and gleaming in the rosy glow
    of twilight's charming hour, the sea-gulls glide
On flapping wings at ease, high in the air,
    Or stand in rows all silent, side by side,
Watching and waiting for their evening fare.

Alone and grand, from out the white sea foam,
    Old Morro lifts his rugged form on high,
Where fierce, tempestuous winds in fury roam.
    Dauntless he lifts his head toward the sky.
He stands, through storm and sunshine, night and day,
    The firm, grim guardian of the placid bay.

Long may the storm-king howl upon the deep,
    And strew, with helpless wrecks, the sandy shore;
Hurl his wild waves about old Morro's feet,
    And fill the air with wild, incessant, roar,
But firm and staunch, through danger's deafening din
    Stands the bold sentry of the bay within.

                      —C. Elwoods
              1800s, exact date unknown

though, also recognized the monolith's uniqueness and qualified his statement by adding, "It is to be hoped, however, that the grandeur and symmetrical proportions of this mass will not be marred, as equally good material can be obtained from the other buttes." He referred, of course, to the other *morros* in the chain. Unfortunately, his advice was not heeded and blasting—which continued intermittently until 1963, providing rock to build and repair Morro Bay's own breakwater in 1942 and 1963—did, indeed, alter and mar the symmetry of the rock forever. (It is estimated that over one million, two hundred thousand tons of rock was blasted from the flanks of the venerable giant during the course of quarrying operations. In 1963, a quarry executive estimated that, all told, the rock could produce over 20 billion tons of building material.)

In 1963, public pressure—applied by local citizens who were outraged at the continued destruction of what a turn-of-the-century news reporter termed "the gray old sentinel who so faithfully guards Pacific's gateway to our little village"—put an end to the blasting at Morro Rock. Then, in 1966, a bill introduced by Assemblyman Burt L. Talcott and Senator Thomas H. Kuchel transferred full title of the historic monolith to the State of California. Kuchel, while urging the bill's passage, said, "This law will enable the people of the United States, now and in the future, to see a unique part of the earth's geography retained in perpetuity for the benefit of all Americans." Finally, in 1968—thanks to the efforts of the Morro Bay Chamber of Commerce and the San Luis Obispo County Historical Society—Morro Rock was officially declared California Registered Historical Landmark Number

The quarry at Morro Rock c. 1890-1895. Courtesy San Luis Obispo County Historical Museum.

The Morro Bay breakwater is constructed of giant boulders blasted from Morro Rock.

821. Since then, it has been protected from all but the forces of nature.

Following construction of the causeway in 1936, Morro Rock's accessibility made it a popular spot with picnickers who used steps carved in the rock and a well-marked trail to reach its summit. In 1973, though, the California Department of Fish and Game, in cooperation with the State Department of Parks and Recreation, banned climbing and declared the Rock an ecological preserve (now called the Morro Rock Natural Preserve), a refuge for a nesting pair of endangered peregrine falcons. (Note: The "no climbing" ban is still in effect and is very strictly enforced. Perpetrators are subject to immediate discipline and a heavy fine.) Today, the Morro Rock falcons—with the help of the Predatory Bird Research Group at the University of California at Santa Cruz and the protection of the Department of Fish and Game—prosper near the food-rich bay and raise their young on a stone ledge 300 feet above the surf that has buffeted the sides of their home for millions of years.

God's Pyramid

Where rolling sand dunes stretch away
By Morro's blue and quiet bay
And this child of Old Ocean's pride
Clings fondly to its mother's side;

Where gardens from the friendly shore
Send sweetly scented greetings o'er;
Where wearied sea birds nightly flock—
All, all alone stands Morro Rock.

The mountains, rising far away,
All seem to scorn her by the Bay
And dim and lofty thru the haze
To look at her in dumb amaze.

Could faithful annals better show
How vain a feeble Pharaoh?
No lash was used no treasures hid
While building this—God's pyramid.

Her slopes would scarce a lichen grow
And man's abode can never know,
For he must deem himself content
If he may scale her steep ascent

To carve his name in bold relief
Far, far above the rocky reef
And hope that in some future age
They'll note his strut across the stage.

If evened out and tilled with care
E'en steeps like these might fruitage bear,
Then pause my friend and reason why
This lofty peak should pierce the sky.

You'll find that every rock and race
Has in His plan a proper place—
Hers—just to stand within the sea
And teach to men humility.

—Delmar H. Williams
Date Unknown

Back from the Ledge of Extinction

The American peregrine falcon—once largely distributed in the United States, then reduced to a total country-wide population of just 100 mating pairs—has made a remarkable comeback. Today ornithologists estimate that there are 540 falcon pairs in the United States. Ninety of those rule the skies of California (in 1975 there were only eight pairs in the state) and 12 pairs—the Morro Rock pair being the most famous—nest along the coast from Monterey to Pismo Beach.

The decline in population was due mainly to the pesticide DDT which entered the falcon's system when it fed on smaller animals infected with the poison. The result was infertile or thin-shelled eggs. But, falconers—who prized the birds for their speed and the ease with which they were trained—were also responsible because they robbed many nests of the chicks that did hatch.

The comeback began about 15 years ago when scientists and conservationists perfected nest manipulation and captive breeding techniques and implemented recovery programs nationwide. In California—and, specifically, at Morro Rock—the program is administered by the Predatory Bird Research Group at the University of California at Santa Cruz in cooperation with the California Department of Fish and Game.

Peregrines—master aerobats and hunters—have been known to nest on Morro Rock's craggy ledges since the late 1960s. But, though federally protected as an endangered species, they suffered at the hands of man. Blasting at the Rock caused one pair to abandon its nest. Another pair left apparently because of too much human activity. Then, in 1972, authorities apprehended falconers who—on two occasions—had robbed the nest of young birds.

In 1973, the California Department of Fish and Game in cooperation with the California Department of Parks and Recreation, declared Morro Rock an ecological preserve. This move made climbing strictly illegal, punishable by immediate arrest, heavy fine and possible imprisonment. The official announcement read, "This action should assure these peregrines the opportunity to successfully nest and bring forth their young, protected as they are from human encroachment." A year later, thanks to funds donated by the Defenders of Wildlife and the National Audubon Society, an electronic device was installed on the Rock to aid in the detection of trespassers and the enforcement of the ordinance.

The Morro Bay State Park Museum of Natural History maintains an excellent exhibit on the Morro Rock peregrine falcons.

Today the Morro Rock falcons are fiercely protected by residents as well as law officials and, during the nesting season, the nest—and the birds—are watched constantly. According to scientists at the Predatory Bird Research Group, the eggs in the Morro Rock nest still suffer from the effects of DDT. So, the eggs are removed each year (they are replaced with infertile eggs so that the mother will continue nesting) and taken to the Santa Cruz facility for incubation. Once hatched, the young chicks are returned to the nest where mom and dad care for them until they can manage on their own.

Those involved in peregrine research are very encouraged by the birds' comeback and hope that, in five to seven years, they can be "downlisted" from endangered to threatened. Until then, these magnificent birds of prey—including the pair who call Morro Rock home—will continue to get a helping hand from man who, ironically, is the one responsible for their near extinction.

The House that Criddle Built

In the 1940s, Arthur Criddle—a Morro Bay resident who discovered the bayside village in the 1920s—was part of the work crew that blasted twenty-ton boulders from Morro Rock to build the harbor breakwaters. He was fascinated with the beautiful multicolored stone—the cuts revealed shades of yellow, blue, brown, white and more—and got permission to haul away some the the scraps. When—pick-up truckload by pick-up truckload—he'd collected enough, he began work on his now-famous house.

Criddle—who had never worked with stone and who says the blueprints were in his head, not on paper—hand split about 500 tons of rock and pieced it together to form the veneer. Behind it he built an inner wall of concrete and steel. The roof is supported by stout 16x16-inch Douglas fir timbers salvaged from the railroad trestle that was built by the Army Corps of Engineers to facilitate the quarrying operations. Each of the 22 windows—and the massive fireplace and chimney—is trimmed with white limestone he quarried at Lime Mountain on the Santa Rita Grade.

Criddle and his family moved into their new home on Thanksgiving Day, 1947—after a four-and-a-half-year labor of love—and lived there until 1973 when he sold his one-of-a-kind dream house to a restaurateur. Today, the Criddle home—located at 2738 North Main Street—houses Dutch's Fine Dining. There have been some changes made—most notable, the addition of the red tile walkway, the awning above the entrance and the shubbery that hides much of the stonework. But, underneath it all, it's still the house that Criddle built—a testament to an ancient landmark and the man who saw in it a delicate beauty lost to those who appreciated only the mass and weight of the boulders it produced.

The historic Criddle House—now home to Dutch's Fine Dining.

The Legend of Morro Castle

The following is a story spun by a "Passing Traveler" and related by Myron Angel in his *History of San Luis Obispo County—1883*. There are other legends—including a fanciful tale about a hermit who makes his home inside Morro Rock, a giant geode. But this is the most widely told—and the most romantic—for it features a promi-

nent Morro Bay historic figure and explains the cloud of fog that often hovers over the Rock, hiding its summit. Whether fact or fiction, it's a tribute to the men and women who, throughout the centuries, have loved this volcano-turned-landmark and who recognize in it a timeless beauty.

"Only 10 or 12 miles from San Luis Obispo is Morro Bay, the estero of the old Spaniards, and laid down on the maps as Estero Bay.

The curiosity I felt to see this place was not, I confess, so much due to what was told me of its importance as a bay and a point of geographical and commercial importance, as the bit of romance connected with a rock rising abruptly out of the midst of the harbor. ... "...The story which, to me, threw such a halo around Morro Rock, a cone-shaped, symmetrical mass of reddish color, lifting itself about 200 feet out to the dashing waves, runs as follows:

A Spaniard had conceived such a love for this lonely, sea-washed pile that he built himself a house a few miles inland, called it Morro Castle, and made a dying request that his body should be carried to the top of the rock and buried among the jutting crags and scant vegetation.

Truly, the old Spaniard had grand ideas, for what monument could be raised to man more imperishable than this rock, looming up so darkly from the bosom of the blue waters, where the sea bird with its restless cry, and the winds with deep-rolling voice, could intone eternal requiems over him.

Wherever his body may have been laid, his spirit seems not to have found rest; for it is said that strange noises are heard around the house he built, and slow, stealthy steps measure the length of the garret and seem to descend to the ground outside.

... The stairway leading to the garret is on the outside of the house. ... The present owner assured us that he seldom entered this place, and that he had done nothing to have it cleared of debris he found there.

Moth-eaten remnants of gay, rich Spanish costumes were lying in curious heaps on the floor, and old saddles, bridles and spurs were slowly mouldering into dust; but I could well fancy how these garments resumed their former glitter when at midnight they clothed again the supple form of the proud Spaniard, and how this fiery steed found his way out of the hills to carry his master in one mad gallop down to the Morro Rock...."

Note: "Morro Castle" is the Anglicized name given to the Canet adobe—*Moro Casa*—built in 1841 by Vincente Canet, owner of the San Bernardo Rancho. It still stands in the middle of a dairy farm on Adobe

Road, east of Highway 1 between San Bernardo and San Luisito Creek Roads. Legend has it that the ghost rider is Vincente Canet himself and, that when he reaches the shore, his spirit takes the form of a cloud of fog and hovers over the Rock he loved so dearly.

The "True" Story of Morro Rock

Reprinted with the permission of Harold Wieman who spun the story in the September 4, 1975, issue of the Morro Bay Sun Bulletin

It has been said that Morro Rock is of volcanic origin, but that does not tell the whole story. The real truth is that what we call Morro Rock is a giant geoduck clam, a remnant of the dinosaur age that was entrapped by a flow of lava.

When you get to thinking about it, it is no wonder that the Morro Bay monster has gone unrecognized for so long. Aerial photographs, a comparatively recent tool for studying the earth's phenomena, clearly show the round shell shape with the long siphon extending out to sea. That is one point and another is that the study of marine invertebrate zoology has taught us that many sea worms protect themselves from observation and predation with an encrusting layer of rock. Phragmatopoma californica (sandcastle worm), for example, secretes mucus that cements particles of sand around its body. This kind of protection is not unusual in nature.

But now that the Great Morro Geoduck (pronounced "gooey duck") at the entrance to the bay has been identified, a lot of other things become comprehensible. Take the tides.

The huge clam siphon extending out to sea draws in water and causes the water to pour out of the bay exposing the mud flats. After the clam has extracted the food, water gushes out of the siphon and the bay is filled once again.

All these years we have watched the tide surging in and out of the bay and have turned to science for the explanation. And scien-

tists, not wanting to appear ignorant, have tried to explain the tides. They say the moon does it. Now who could believe that?

The existence of sea monsters has been common knowledge since sailors sailed their ships to the ends of the earth. ... But in these days of enlightenment, monsters are no longer creatures that cause fear and trembling. Things like monsters and ghosts have been used for very practical purposes. In England the sight-seeing tours include, among other things, the Ghost of the Leicesterhamsteadshire (pronounced "Lesser") Castle. In Scotland tourists come to see the home of the Loch Ness Dragon. Alaskans like to point out Lake Illiamna where the monster rises from the deep at mealtimes and swallows whole caribous.

A local monster can be of economic value, however, only if it stays put.

Paul Bunyan, the Abominable Snowman and Bigfoot have indeed become legendary, but they are of no value to local chambers of commerce because they have become afflicted with the wanderlust....

Therefore, it is reassuring to know that our own local monster is of the kind that will stay put. We depend on the Great Morro Geoduck to stay right where it is out on Coleman Drive, forcing water in and out of its huge siphon, keeping the tides flowing in and out of the bay.

Davidson Seamount

lthough sketchy information concerning the exceedingly irregular configuration of the ocean bottom off the California Coast has been available since early days and scrutiny of the land contours immediately adjacent to the coast shows that much irregularity is to be expected, it is only during the past few years and in the process of executing modern hydrographic surveys that the full extent of this irregularity has been appreciated. The execution of an accurate and complete survey in such an area tests to the very limit the adequacy of our most modern equipment and the cooperative skill of the personnel engaged.

— F.L. Peacock
United States Coast and Geodetic Survey, 1932

These are the opening words of a bulletin published in December, 1932, by the United States Coast and Geodetic Survey detailing the work of its survey ship *Guide*. It was in 1932 that, during their voyages along the California coast, scientists on the *Guide* discovered an undersea mountain west of Morro Rock. The mountain, according to a National Oceanic and Atmospheric Administration official, was about 7,800 feet high with its summit about 3,600 feet below the surface of the water and was a significant find.

It was not until 1938, however, that this

great undersea mountain was named Davidson Seamount in honor of George Davidson, a leading scientist in the fields of geodesy and geography who, in 1850, had participated in the first official survey of the Pacific Coast. During his fifty years of service to the United States Coast Survey (designated the United States Coast and Geodetic Survey in 1878 and the National Oceanic and Atmospheric Administration in 1970), Davidson became the leading expert on California's offshore terrain.

The name Davidson Seamount was important for another reason also, for this was the first time that the word "seamount" had been used to describe an undersea geographic feature. According to the Coast and Geodetic Survey, "the generic term 'seamount' is here used for the first time and is applied to submarine elevations of mountain form whose character and depth are such that bank, shoal, pinnacle, etc. are not appropriate." (Note: The National Oceanic and Atmospheric Administration is celebrating the 100th anniversary of the Board of Geodetic Names in 1990 by publishing a commemorative map of the Davidson Seamount. The honor recognizes the submarine mountain's distinction as being the first to be designated a "seamount.")

Although they have not been able to test their assumptions, geologists believe that the Davidson Seamount is of the same origin as San Luis Obispo County's *morros*—one that formed and remained underwater. Beyond that, all is speculation. Still, it's fun to imagine a submerged *morro* whose nooks and crannies shelter unfamiliar creatures of the deep—perhaps very similar to those who called it home 25 million years ago.

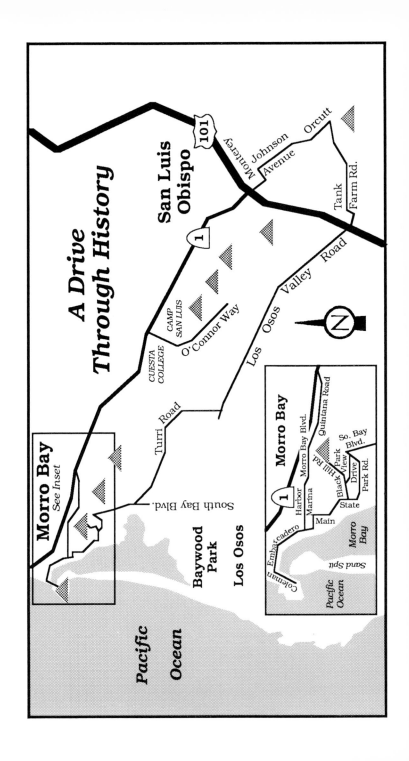

A Drive
Through History

San Luis
Obispo

101

Monterey
Johnson
Avenue
Orcutt
Tank
Farm Rd.

1

CAMP
SAN LUIS

O'Connor Way

Los Osos Valley Road

N

CUESTA
COLLEGE

Turri Road

South Bay Blvd.

Baywood
Park

Los Osos

Morro Bay
See Inset

Pacific
Ocean

Morro Bay

Quintana Road

Morro Bay Blvd.

Hill Rd.

So. Bay
Blvd.

1

Harbor

Black
Marina

Park
View

Drive

Park Rd.

State

Embarcadero

Main

Coleman

Morro
Bay

Sand Spit

Pacific
Ocean

A Drive Through History

*he principal physical feature (of San
Luis Obispo County) is the Santa
Lucia Range of mountains, running
nearly parallel with the coast, dividing the county
into unequal parts, each of distinctive characteris-
tics. ... From Estero Bay the Mount Buchon Range
extends southeastward a distance of about twenty
miles.... Between these ranges is a succession of
detached buttes, as the Mission and Bishop's
Peaks, near the town of San Luis Obispo, having an
elevation of 1,500 and 1,800 feet. This range of
buttes terminates on the northeast* (sic) *in Moro
Rock, in the Estero Bay; and in the southeast,
gradually sink in low, scattered hills.*

—Myron Angel
History of San Luis Obispo County, 1883

In Angel's day, the horseback or buggy ride
from Islay Hill to Morro Rock and back was possible, but not practical. Buttes or no buttes, it was
definitely not the kind of thing people did for diver-
sion on a Sunday afternoon. Instead, turn-of-the-
century county residents and visitors enjoyed the
majesty of close-in San Luis Mountain (what Angel
referred to as Mission Peak) and Bishop Peak. And,
when it was time for a trip to the seashore, they
marveled at Morro Rock. They missed something,
though, for although each individual peak is special, it is the linear chain that makes the *morros*

geologic and scenic wonders.

Today a driving tour of the *morros* is not only practical, it's pleasurable. Time permitting, it can take the better part of a day—with stops for shopping, eating and sightseeing—or, if time is short, it can be completed in just a couple of hours. Either way, driving (or bicycling) from one end of the chain of *morros* and back is an experience in beauty and history that shouldn't be missed.

Start the tour at the intersection of Orcutt and Tank Farm Roads southeast of downtown San Luis Obispo (see map on page 75). Set your odometer at 0.0 then head west on Tank Farm Road. At this point, Islay Hill—the southernmost of the *morros* —is directly to the left. According to a local historian, the name *Islay* is derived from the Salinan Indian word *slay* (pronounced "sly") meaning wild cherry (Prunus ilicifolia), sometimes called choke cherry because birds choke on the seeds. Pedro Fages—a military lieutenant who accompanied Portolá on his trek up the coast in 1769—recorded the word as *yslay* in his journal and from that came the Anglicized spelling. (Note: Today county residents pronounce the word "iss´- lay.")

Islay Hill—chapparal-covered with barely a rock protruding to betray its violent origin—is at the northwest boundary of the 30,911-acre Corral de Piedra Rancho granted to Maria Francisca Rafaela Isabel Rodriguez and her husband José Maria Villavicencia in 1841. In 1858 the family built an adobe home at the base of Islay Hill and, since the rancho was passed down through the Rodriguez family, that building became known as the Rodriguez Adobe. It still stands—surrounded by a chain link fence—in the midst of a new housing

The Rodriguez Adobe was built on the Corral de Piedra Rancho in 1858. Photo c. 1930. Courtesy San Luis Obispo County Historical Museum.

The adobe still stands today. If all goes according to plan, it will soon be restored and will be surrounded by a public park.

development. City and county residents and officials, together with groups such as the Cultural
Heritage Commission of the city San Luis Obispo
and the San Luis Obispo County Historical Society,
protested when it appeared that the adobe was in
jeopardy of being demolished to make way for new
houses. Those protests led to an agreement with
Pacifica Corporation, the developer of the estates at
the base of the hill. It has agreed to provide some
funds for the restoration of the adobe and to surround it by a public park. _(As this book went to
press, the adobe was still in disrepair and the details of the restoration and park had not been final-
ized. However, the adobe is visible from Sunflower
Street. To see it, turn left on Morning Glory Way
(about .1 mile west of the railroad overpass), left
again on Fuller Road, then right on Sunflower
Street. Follow Sunflower to the end. The adobe is to
the southeast near the railroad tracks.)_

Continue west on Tank Farm Road. Mine Hill
(aka Righetti Hill) is on the right at .1 miles. This is
a minor member of the volcanic chain and was
mined for chromium during the 1890s. The mine—
and the road leading up to it—is clearly visible
about halfway up the west slope of the hill.

Stay on Tank Farm Road and cross Highway
227/Broad Street (1.0). At 1.4 miles, San Luis
Mountain is clearly visible on the right at about 2
o'clock. It's easy to spot, it's the one with the road
ringing it from top to bottom. At this point, Bishop
Peak is hidden, but Cerro Romualdo (look for a
very conical summit) and Hollister Peak are visible
in the distance to the north. As you near South
Higuera Street (2.8), Bishop Peak (look for the
three points on the summit) comes out from under

Workers constructing the one million barrel tank at the San Luis Obispo Tank Farm c. 1913. The tank farm was the site of an infamous fire in 1926. Note Islay Hill in the distance on the right and Mine Hill on the left. Courtesy San Luis Obispo County Historical Museum.

San Luis Mountain's shadow. (Note: The oil tank farm along this stretch has a long history. See the photograph above for details.)

Turn left on South Higuera Street and stay in the right hand lane. Then, turn right on Los Osos Valley Road (3.2). At the Highway 101 overpass (3.5), look to the right. San Luis Mountain, Bishop Peak, Chumash Peak and Cerro Romualdo (from south to north) are all very prominent. Cross Madonna Road (4.6), staying on Los Osos Valley Road. This residential section of the city is referred to as the Laguna Lake area, named for the lake—*La Laguna*—and the rancho granted to the Church in 1844. At this point the peaks are on the right, but they are partially hidden by trees, houses and condominiums.

The clutter starts to break up at 5.1 miles and San Luis Mountain, Bishop Peak and Chumash Peak (from south to north) form a dramatic

backdrop for Laguna Junior High School on the
right. A bit further down (5.7), broad-based San
Luis Mountain is directly on the right. At Foothill
Boulevard (6.4) you leave the city behind and pastureland and rolling foothills surround the four
giants: San Luis Mountain (for historic details see
pages 36-45) at 3 o'clock, Bishop Peak (for historic
details see pages 46-57) and Chumash Peak at 2
o'clock and Cerro Romualdo at 1 o'clock.

Chumash Peak is adjacent to Bishop Peak
and is 1,257 feet high. It is composed of a number
of very large boulders and can be identified by the
prominent knob of stone (a huge boulder) that
decorates its northern exposure. Louisiana Clayton
Dart—longtime county resident and past curator of
the San Luis Obispo County Historical Museum—
named the peak in 1964 in honor of the Chumash
Indians who were such an important part of San
Luis Obispo County history. She said of the knob
which identifies the peak, "... one can easily imagine an alert Indian standing there long ago, scan-
ning the horizon for friend or foe—or game."

Dart intervened in the naming of this peak
(and Cerro Cabrillo) when she learned that the
Department of the Interior's Board on Geographic
Names was proposing to name them both after Los
Angeles citizens. Dart received official notice that
her proposed names had been adopted in November, 1964. In that letter, the Board on Geographic
Names noted that Chumash Peak would be officially recognized as a "peak with an elevation of
about 1,250 feet, just northwest of Bishop Peak
and about 2 miles north-northwest of San Luis
Obispo; named for a linguistic family of Indians
that lived on the south coast of California...." At

7.0 miles, Chumash Peak is at 3 o'clock. From this angle it looks completely different than it did at Foothill Boulevard.

Soon after passing Foothill Boulevard, San Luis Mountain, Bishop Peak and Chumash Peak are left behind and Cerro Romualdo becomes the prominent landmark. It's easy to identify because of its very conical shape rising to a single point at the summit. This peak has been known by its present name since 1842 when Romualdo—the only Chumash Indian to receive a Mexican land grant following the secularization of the missions— was granted 117 acres at its base. It rises 1,306 feet above the land he called *Huerta de Romualdo*— Romualdo's kitchen garden or orchard. Romualdo sold his land to Captain John Wilson—owner of the massive 32,622-acre Cañada de los Osos y Pecho y Islay Rancho—in 1846. Although it had a succession of owners, it is unique among the ranchos in that it remained one unit—i.e it was not subdivided or swallowed up by a larger holding— until 1941 when the property was sold to the State of California and became part of Camp San Luis Obispo. Cerro Romualdo is still on camp property and is used by California National Guard troops for fitness training—the heavy combat boots have trampled a well-worn path to its summit—and target practice.

Cerro Romualdo was quarried in the 1890s for rock which was used in the construction of the Southern Pacific Railroad in San Luis Obispo County. According to the 1896 edition of the California State Mining Bureau's *State Mineralogist Report* and the same bureau's *The Structural and Industrial Materials of California* published in 1906, this quarry—known as Lee's Quarry—was on the north face of the mountain at about 625 foot elevation and yielded a hard, light gray porphyry which was supposedly used in the trimmings of the old San Luis Obispo courthouse (now demolished) and in railway culverts and bridges. The quarry has been idle since 1891. However, in the early 1970s, the land owner petitioned the San Luis Obispo County Planning Commission for permission to open a new quarry on the Los Osos Valley side of the mountain. The planners rejected the proposal due to the protests of a number of environmental groups and private citizens who were intent on preserving the scenic beauty of the *morros*.

At 8.0 miles, all but Cerro Romualdo's summit is hidden by the rolling foothills in the foreground. Then, at 9.3 miles (road sign reads "Lane Ends Merge Left"), 1,404-foot Hollister Peak—composed of very large boulders—towers over the landscape on the right at about 2 o'clock. Although this is not the highest of the *morros*—Bishop Peak has that honor—it is definitely the most magnificent and awesome. According to the Sierra Club's *San Luis Obispo County Trail Guide*, golden eagles are often seen soaring around Hollister's summit and have been known to nest there.

Turn right on Turri Road (10.6). Hollister Peak is now in front at about 11 o'clock, framed by rolling foothills. Keep an eye on this peak as the road curves and climbs. Originally called *Cerro Alto*—high mountain—it was renamed for Joseph and Ellen Hollister who bought the San Luisito and El Chorro Ranchos in 1865. From that time on, these two properties were known as the Hollister Homestead and the mountain became Hollister

Hollister Peak's rocky summit.

Peak. The Hollister family moved into and enlarged an adobe home which was built by Guadalupe Cantua—the original grantee of the San Luisito Rancho—about 1841. (It still stands on the Cuesta College campus and will be highlighted during the drive south on Highway 1.)

Turri Road twists and turns and rolls up and down, offering fantastic views of Hollister Peak. Then, at 12.5 miles No Name Hill comes into view at about 2 o'clock and Cerro Cabrillo at about 1 o'clock. Cabrillo—which is actually two peaks of nearly equal height—is composed of many small boulders. It is 911 feet at its highest point and was named by Louisiana Clayton Dart in 1964 (at the same time she named Chumash Peak). Dart named the peak in honor of Juan Rodríguez Cabrillo—she referred to him as "the intrepid Portuguese explorer who was sailing under the flag of Spain..."—who, in 1542, sailed into Estero Bay and christened the rock near the shore *El Morro*. In its letter to Dart confirming her proposed name, the Board on Geographic Names said, "The decision will be promulgated in Decision List 6403 as follows: Cabrillo, Cerro: mountain peak with an elevation of about 912 feet, about 1.3 miles southeast of the town of Morro Bay; named for Juan Rodríguez Cabrillo, a Portuguese navigator in Spanish service, who, in 1542, was commander of the first expedition to sail along the coast of California...."

Today, most of Cerro Cabrillo is within the boundaries of Morro Bay State Park. There is a trail leading to its summit—the highest point in the State Park—which is popular with hikers and rock climbers. It is not, however, an official State Park trail. (For access details, see page 111.) Those exploring Cabrillo on foot will find an idle quarry (details unknown) on Cabrillo's south side and a gravel pit on its northwest side. Between Cerro Cabrillo and Hollister Peak there is an 811-foot hill which is believed to be of the same origin as the *morros*. It however, remains unnamed and local residents refer to it, appropriately, as No Name Hill.

Follow Turri Road to South Bay Boulevard (15.3)—by now you've already had your first view of Morro Rock in the distance—and turn right. As you make the turn, Cerro Cabrillo is directly ahead—its base in the salt marsh—and 665-foot Black Hill is at 11 o'clock. For a good look at Cabrillo's boulders, pull over in the turnout at 16.0 miles, then continue north on South Bay Boulevard and turn left on State Park Road (16.7).

Chaparral-covered Black Hill is now directly on the right. It is within Morro Bay State Park boundaries and is the most accessible of all of the *morros*. (Despite extensive research, its name remains a mystery—at least to this author. It's possible that it was named for the color of its rock, although this is doubtful because its exposed surfaces are weathered to almost white.) At 16.8 miles, veer right at the Y onto Park View Drive, a route which leads to the Morro Bay State Park Golf Course and, eventually, to the summit of Black Hill.

Morro Bay State Park is 1,905 acres of tree-shaded campgrounds and developed areas, rolling hills, wetlands and primitive natural reserves. In the early 1900s, the area you are driving through was farmed by John Schneider, a Morro Bay pioneer. In addition to hay, he planted the eucalyptus trees that enhance the area to this day. Two decades later, land developers discovered this bayside paradise. They built a nine-hole golf course, stables, bridle paths, tennis courts and an exclusive clubhouse which overlooked the golf links. The idea, of course, was to induce inland residents to buy property and build vacation and permanent homes. Plans for the residential development fizzled during the Depression years and, in 1934, the financially troubled developers sold the golf course, White's Point (where the Museum of Natural History now stands), the campground area and Black Hill to the State of California for a total of $250,000. Young men from the Civilian Conservation Corps built the new state park campground—including the beautiful masonry drainage ditches that line State Park Road, Park View Drive and Black Hill Road. The state has made many improvements to the park over the years—including the expansion of the golf course from nine to eighteen holes and the addition of a marina and a natural history museum.

Turn right on Black Hill Road at about 17.4 miles. (This is a tricky, unmarked intersection and easily missed because it looks more like a golf cart trail than a road. If you get to the clubhouse you have gone too far. Fortunately, there's a large parking lot where you can turn around.) Black Hill Road literally winds through the golf course then dead ends at a parking area (18.3). The view from here is absolutely marvelous with Morro Bay harbor, the Rock, the back bay, the salt marsh, the sand spit and the Pacific Ocean stealing the show. But, if you're willing to hike a bit, it gets much better. Follow the short, well-maintained trail to the summit. Once there, you'll be rewarded with a bird's eye view of the north coast and the *morros* trailing back to San Luis Obispo.

Looking over the salt marsh toward the Los Osos/Baywood Park area from the summit of Black Hill.

After you've enjoyed the view, retrace your steps to the intersection of Park View Drive and Black Hill Road (19.0), bear right, proceed past the clubhouse to State Park Road (19.3), then turn right. Once outside of the State Park boundary, State Park Road becomes Main Street. Morro Rock is now unmistakable on your left. Turn left on Marina Street (20.2), follow it to Embarcadero (20.3) and turn right.

This bustling waterfront is where Morro Bay began. In 1864, Franklin Riley discovered that the area was between the boundaries of the San Bernardo and Moro y Cayucos Ranchos and, thus, open to homesteading. He claimed 160 acres and, in 1870, began laying out the town of Moro. Two years later he built the town's first wharf. The town grew quickly in the 1870s as schooners thronged to Riley's wharf to pick up wool, produce and dairy products. But the harbor entrance was treacherous and captains feared the high surf, surging tides and erratic winds. By the turn of the century, many ships bypassed Moro (the second "r" was added in the late 1800s although Cabrillo originally called the Rock *El Morro*) in favor of a new wharf at nearby Cayucos. The embarcadero continued to thrive, though, thanks to a prosperous commercial fishing industry. Today it is a pleasant mix of people and businesses who make their living from the sea, small shops and eateries.

After you've made the stop at Beach Street (20.7), continue northwest on Embarcadero. There's no mistaking Morro Rock now so just follow your nose past the Pacific Gas and Electric Company Power Plant (20.9 on the right) and the

continued on page 98

Top and bottom: Islay Hill from Orcutt Road east of its intersection with Tank Farm Road.

San Luis Mountain from Los Osos Valley Road.

San Luis Mountain from Highway 1.

Bishop Peak from Los Osos Valley Road.

Bishop Peak from Highway 1.

Chumash Peak from Los Osos Valley Road.

Chumash Peak from Highway 1.

Cerro Romualdo from Los Osos Valley Road.

Cerro Romualdo from Highway 1.

Hollister Peak from Turri Road.

Hollister Peak from Highway 1.

Cerro Cabrillo from South Bay Boulevard.

Cerro Cabrillo from Quintana Road.

Black Hill from South Bay Boulevard..

Black Hill from Quintana Road..

Morro Rock from Embarcadero.

Morro Rock from Morro Strand State Beach.

Coast Guard (21.0 on the left). Embarcadero becomes Coleman Drive as it makes the turn west at
21.1 miles. From here to the Rock you are driving
over the causeway built in 1930s by the Works
Progress Administration to connect the Rock to
shore and facilitate quarrying operations. This
closed the north entrance to the harbor, but the
Army Corps of Engineers dredged a new south
channel and, with help from the WPA, built a
breakwater to protect its entrance. In the early
1940s, a south breakwater was built and the north
breakwater was improved. All of these projects
used rock quarried from Morro Rock. (For historic
details, see pages 58-72.)

Quarrying stopped at Morro Rock in the
early 1960s and, in 1968, the Rock was declared
an official state landmark (Number 821). The
plaque commemorating that event is on the right
at 21.4 miles and is mounted on a piece of the old
monolith itself. Continue your drive past the Rock
to the end of the road (21.7) at the north breakwater. From here you'll have a wonderful close-up
look at the Rock and the harbor entrance. The
Rock is a natural preserve for the peregrine falcons
which nest on its rocky ledges (see pages 66-67)
and is strictly off limits to hikers. But you can walk
around its base, touching the stone which formed
in the bowels of the earth 25 million years ago.

When you're ready to continue your drive,
backtrack to Beach Street (22.8) then stay on
Embarcadero until you reach Harbor Street (22.9)
and turn left. Follow Harbor Street to Morro Bay
Boulevard (23.5), turn left, then right on Quintana
Road (23.7). At about 24.3 miles, Black Hill, Cerro
Cabrillo and Hollister Peak (from north to south)

are visible on the right with Hollister being the most prominent at about 1 o'clock. Cross South Bay Boulevard (24.7) and continue south on Quintana Road. This stretch of road, fronting Highway 1, is agricultural and, with nothing to block your view, you get a marvelous look at Cerro Cabrillo's two summits and at the bouldery facade of Hollister Peak. According to county historian Louisiana Clayton Dart, Hollister is sometimes referred to as the Holy Mountain because of an illusion created by a grouping of about 12 boulders at its summit. If your imagination is good, you may see a nativity scene complete with a veiled Mary holding the baby Jesus while Joseph looks on. (This illusion is better from the northbound lane of Highway 1.) Another picture which some people see in the rocks on Hollister's eastern slope is that of a small boy being chased by a harbor seal. Still another is a scowling old man. That one, by the way, is apparent on our cover photograph. Use your imagination and many pictures will unfold in the rocks.

Quintana Road joins Highway 1 at 25.7 miles. (Note: The Canet Adobe, the subject of _The Legend of Morro Castle_ on page 71, is across the highway. To see it, cross to San Bernardo Creek Road and turn right on Adobe Road. The adobe— now a private home and looking quite modern—is down the road on the left in the middle of a dairy farm.) Turn right (south) and look in your rearview mirror for a parting view of Morro Rock. Hollister Peak now dominates the landscape to the right, sweeping down to the highway with several small farms at its base. If you're up to a short sidetrip, turn right on Canet Road (27.1) and follow it to a suspension bridge spanning Chorro Creek. To the

Craggy Hollister Peak framed by a suspension bridge on Canet Road.

south, you'll get a unique look at Hollister Peak. In lieu of the sidetrip (or after it), continue south on Highway 1. In December, 1988, a developer proposed building 300 housing units and a golf course on this side of Hollister Peak. The proposal fizzled, however, and most San Luis Obispo County residents hope that the land ringing this mighty peak will remain agricultural. At 27.6 miles, Cerro Romualdo is directly ahead with Chumash Peak to the south. As you leave Hollister behind, look to the right. The small farm (27.8) at about 2 o'clock is protected by two sugarloafs of the same volcanic rock that forms the *morros*. This farm has been in the same family since the late 1800s.

As you drive south on Highway 1, Cerro Romualdo and Chumash Peak (north to south) are the dominant landmarks and, at 30.1 miles (north entrance to Cuesta College) they form a dramatic background for the college and Camp San Luis

Obispo. Turn right at the south entrance to Cuesta College (30.6) and follow Hollister Road along the south side of the campus to Chorro Valley Road (31.0). The small building on the southwest corner of this intersection is the Hollister Adobe, built in 1841 by Guadalupe Cantua. It became the home of the Joseph Hollister family in 1866. The Hollisters raised six children in the home, adding a room with each new pint-sized addition. Eventually, a comfortable ranch home—which was a center for San Luis Obispo County social, political and business activity—encircled the original small adobe. Three generations of Hollisters lived in the adobe until, in 1907, the family was forced to leave because of financial difficulties brought on by severe drought. Camillo Ghiringhelli—the next owner of the adobe—willed it to his daughter, Lillie Hansen, and she lived in the comfortable home until 1940 when the War Department bought up much land in the Chorro Valley to expand operations at Camp San Luis Obispo (originally Camp Merriam, home of the California National Guard).

Unfortunately, the Army had no need for the ranch home and bulldozers had demolished all but the original three-room adobe before John Hubbard "Hub" Hollister—who had been raised in the home—persuaded the camp powers that be to save the historic landmark. During World War II, men stationed at the camp attended outdoor church services in the secluded, tree-shaded area surrounding the home. Then, following the war, the site was abandoned and the adobe began to deteriorate badly. In 1967, San Luis Obispo County Junior College (now Cuesta College) bought the land for part of its new campus. By that time, the

The Hollister Adobe—built about 1841—as it appeared c. 1890.
Courtesy San Luis Obispo County Historical Museum.

The restored adobe—minus all of the Hollister family additions—today.

once proud ranch home was in a complete state of disrepair. Doors and windows were broken or non-existent, the walls were crumbling, wood was rotting and there was extensive graffiti and other signs of vandalism.

Thanks to a push by the Cuesta College Board of Trustees, restoration on the Hollister Adobe was begun in 1970—with volunteer help including private citizens, college students and members of the San Luis Obispo County Archaeological Society—and completed in 1973. Today the adobe is recognized as a Point of Historic Interest by the State of California. Maintained by docents of the San Luis Obispo County Archaeological Society, it houses a collection of Chumash Indian artifacts and a small display of Hollister family memorabilia. The museum is open on the first and third Sundays of each month from 1 until 3 pm.

For a close-up look at Cerro Romualdo, Chumash Peak and Bishop Peak, continue southwest on Hollister Road, then turn left at 31.3 miles and left again at the stop sign at 31.5 miles, following the signs to O'Connor Way. This country road winds around Cerro Romualdo then heads south past Chumash and Bishop Peaks. You can take it all the way to Foothill Boulevard, but our tour continues south along Highway 1, so make a U-turn in the Mainini Ranch driveway at 34.1 miles, backtrack to the highway (37.6) and turn right (south). At this point, Cerro Romualdo is directly on the right behind Camp San Luis Obispo. As you pass the camp, look for the combat boot-beaten trail that leads to the summit. Chumash Peak is next and, at 38.4 miles, the knob on its summit is clearly visible at about 1 o'clock.

Once past the camp, the peaks hide behind the foothills until, at about 40.0 miles, Bishop appears at 3 o'clock. After you get a glimpse of Bishop, look straight ahead. At 40.4 miles, the summit of little Islay Hill is visible in the distance. Then, at 40.8 miles, look for the famous Mail Pouch Tobacco Barn with Bishop Peak towering in the background.

This picturesque barn was built in 1895. Over the years, it has been immortalized by countless photographers and artists. But it's more than a pretty face. According to local farmers, the barn—which was used for milking dairy cows—was a modern innovation in a day when the task was generally done outdoors. The rustic relic's main claim to fame today, though, is the sign—"Mail Pouch—Treat Yourself to the Best"—that has graced the moss-covered roof for an undetermined number of years. This early-day billboard was the price the farmer paid to have his barn whitewashed each year. It was a mutually profitable relationship but, in 1946, the ranch's owners were notified that the advertising campaign had been terminated. However, nobody ever painted over the historic sign and, though faded almost beyond recognition, it remains a reminder of a time when high-powered advertising was as simple as a handshake and a yearly coat of paint.

At Highland Drive (42.1), San Luis Mountain is clearly visible at 2 o'clock. You can also see the hiking trail which starts at the south end of Tassajara Drive, leading to its summit. To the left is the entrance to California Polytechnic State University. To the right, Highland Drive leads to the area of Bishop Peak favored by rock climbers.

The Mail Pouch barn—an early-day billboard—has nestled at the base of Bishop Peak since 1895.

Stay on Highway 1—now Santa Rosa Street—and continue southeast past Granite Stairway Mountaineering (43.4), the headquarters for local rock climbers. Turn left on Monterey Street (43.5), then right on Johnson Avenue (43.7). Terrace Hill—a minor member of the chain—is on the right just past Bishop Street (44.6). Stay on

Johnson until it ends at Orcutt Road (45.8) and turn left. Follow Orcutt Road back to your starting point (46.8), using Islay Hill as your guide.

Before you leave the Islay Hill area, drive around to the west (Highway 227) side and take a good look at the face of the hill. If you see the outline of a Christmas tree, it's not an illusion. During the 1987 holiday season, workers for Pacifica Corporation—the housing developers—trampled the brush on the hill in the form of a 200 foot tall Christmas tree. It was intended as a holiday gesture, a gift to the community, but was received like a lump of coal. And, it violated the City's Municipal Code which prohibited any alteration of the hill above the brush line. It turned out to be a mistake, the result of a lack of communication. Nevertheless, tempers flared and the developers were threatened with fines and lawsuits. In the end, Pacifica Corporation readily accepted blame and offered to restore the vegetation.

During the ordeal, San Luis Obispo County residents once again rallied to the defense of their mountains. In a passionate letter to the editor, one citizen whose family had lived in the area for five generations, wrote, "No matter how well-intentioned the disfigurement of Islay Hill may have been, its potential permanence and its total failure to improve on nature is deeply disheartening. Such an act borders on desecration." He closed by saying that punishment was not the answer, though. Instead he hoped that everyone could work together to repair "Islay Hill's lost innocence."

The tree is still there—a scar that man made within just a few hours and one that will take nature years to mend.

Section IV

"We abuse land because we regard it as a commodity belonging to us. When we see land as a community to which we belong, we may begin to use it with love and respect."

—Aldo Leopold

Recreational Access

magine a combination walking-bicycle path on both sides of the sister peaks from San Luis Obispo to Morro Bay. Higher up on the slopes would be trails encircling each sister like a necklace. Ascending to each summit would be a trail for the vigorous. Small campsites would be placed near the natural water sources. Inter-city bus service from San Luis Obispo to Morro Bay would enable people to begin a walk at any point along the way.... Marked natural exhibits would educate the curious. Scout troops could improve their skills. Branch trails would lead to far-off Montaña de Oro to the south and Cerro Alto to the north. These trails would join at Lopez Lake, creating a 50-mile loop around the city. Sounds fantastic. Impossible? No.

—Larry J. Souza

Larry J. Souza—a San Luis Obispeño—recorded these remarks in his journal on February 12, 1971 while relaxing at the summit of Islay Hill. He had just completed a one-day hike that began at sunrise at Morro Rock and ended at dusk on Islay's summit. He closed his journal by saying, "From the summit of Islay at this moment, fog still hides most of the beauty of the land. Much of our outlook is shrouded in the same way. Do what you can as your part in clearing the path to the future."

Souza's dream of a "Nine Sisters Trailway"

has not come true. But, it has not died either. In 1989, the San Luis Obispo County Parks and Recreation Commission began work on a plan for a system of trails throughout the county. At least one of these would provide full access to Bishop Peak. In the meantime, outdoor enthusiasts must be content to hike and bike the few *morros* that are accessible.

The following is a list of the most accessible hiking, cycling and climbing areas. Trailheads are noted on the map on page 110. Of those listed, only the Black Hill, Turtle Rock and Cerro Cabrillo Trails are totally on public land. The others involve varying amounts of trespassing over private land. However, the land owners have graciously adopted a "look-the-other-way" attitude. ***If you choose to hike over private property, you do so at your own risk. Neither the landowners, the author nor the publisher accept any responsibility for the consequences.*** Please respect private property by leaving fences intact and gates closed; packing out what you pack in (and more if there's room for a bit of litter in your day pack); and leaving your dogs behind if you're crossing over areas where cattle are grazing. And, please, do not smoke or build fires. Be aware that ticks and poison oak are prevalent. The best protection is to learn to recognize both and to take precautions like wearing long pants, heavy socks and sturdy shoes.

Trailheads

1. San Luis Mountain — There are several ways to access the trails which lead up to the San Luis Mountain summit. The one most popular with

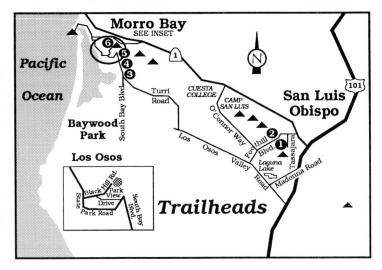

The numbers on this map correspond to the trails described on pages 109-112. Of the trails shown, only those at Cerro Cabrillo (4), Turtle Rock (5) and Black Hill (6) are totally on public land. All others are accessed via private property.

hikers starts at the south end of Tassajara Drive. This is a residential area and parking is available along the street. Another favorite route follows the exercise trail to the north end of Laguna Lake Park, then cuts across pastureland to the mountain. (The departure point from the official trail is easy to recognize. Look for a worn footpath—criss-crossed by fat tire treads—leading east across the pasture.) Both trails require climbing over or through barbed wire fences.

2. Bishop Peak — The easiest hiking access is via Foothill Road. Park on the turnout near This Old House restaurant—about .4 miles southwest of Patricia Drive or 1.3 miles northeast of O'Connor Way. The trail is easily visible from the road. Simply slip through the barbed wire fence and follow the well-worn trail. You can go all the way to the summit for a fantastic view or enjoy a picnic in tree-shaded lower elevations. Rock climbers access a variety of good climbing areas via the south end of Highland Drive. (A pamphlet entitled *Completely Off the Wall: A Climber's Guide to Bishop Peak* is available at Granite Stairway Mountaineering, 871 Santa Rosa Street, San Luis Obispo.)

3. No Name Hill — Hiking access to the trails which ring this hill (some consider it a part of Cerro Cabrillo) is a gate about .3 miles north of Turri Road on the east side of South Bay Boulevard. Look for the turnout on the road and the remains of an old ranch house.

4. Cerro Cabrillo — Hikers and rock climbers access Cerro Cabrillo via two places along the east side of South Bay Boulevard. The first—which leads around the south side of the peak—is a gate at about .3 miles north of Turri Road (same access as No Name Hill). The second is a fence that has been wired open at about .7 miles north of Turri Road. In both cases, there's a turnout that can accommodate a few parked cars. Be certain not to block gates with your car. There are a number of

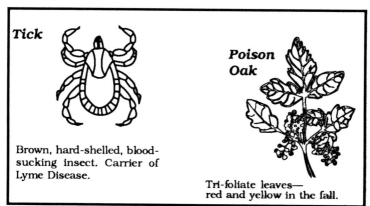

Tick

Brown, hard-shelled, blood-sucking insect. Carrier of Lyme Disease.

Poison Oak

Tri-foliate leaves— red and yellow in the fall.

The view of Cerro Cabrillo and Hollister Peak from Black Hill summit.

trails you can follow. Most start out as dirt roads then narrow to footpaths.

5. Turtle Rock — This small outcropping of rock is on the northwest side of Cerro Cabrillo and there is an official State Park trail leading to the summit. Park in the turnout immediately south of the Twin Bridges Chorro Creek crossing on the east side of South Bay Boulevard, being certain not to block the gate. From there, follow the road behind the gate.

6. Black Hill — Hikers have the choice of following a well-maintained trail which starts near the Morro Bay State Park campground entrance on State Park Road (ask for specific directions at the entrance kiosk) or driving up Black Hill Road to a parking area (see pages 85-87 and 113) and then hiking the remaining few hundred yards to the summit. Either way, the reward is a breathtaking 360-degree view from the top.

Overlooks

Hikers can get a bird's eye view of the chain of *morros* from the summits of San Luis Mountain and Bishop Peak. The less ambitious may want to try these more accessible overlooks. Each affords a marvelous view of the *morros* and the surrounding countryside and each can be reached by vehicle. However, the Cuesta Ridge drive and, to a lesser extent, the drive up to the Prefumo Canyon Road/ See Canyon Road summit, are meant for motorists with a sense of adventure.

1. Cuesta Ridge—From the truck parking area on the west (southbound) side of Highway 101 near the summit of Cuesta Grade, take TV Tower Road to the summit. (Note: This is a narrow, winding dirt road, parts of which are sometimes accessible only to four-wheel drive vehicles. If the going gets too rough, you can park and hike to the summit.)

2. Black Hill Lookout—From State Park Road in Morro Bay State Park, follow Black Hill Road through the golf course to a paved parking area and overlook near the summit of Black Hill. The view from here is marvelous, but it's even better from the summit. If you're up for a short walk, follow the easy, well-maintained trail to the top.

3. Prefumo Canyon Road/See Canyon Road Summit—From the Avila Beach area, take See Canyon Road off of San Luis Bay Drive first through an apple-tree filled canyon then through cattle-grazing land to the summit. (Note: The road

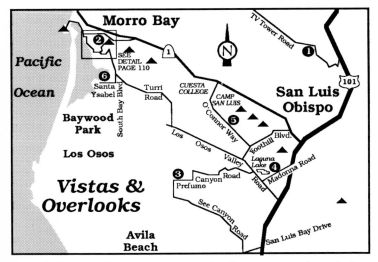

The numbers on this map correspond to the vistas and overlooks described on pages 113-117. The Cuesta Ridge overlook (1) and the Prefumo Canyon Road/See Canyon Road Summit (3) should only be attempted by the adventurous motorist.

is paved for about five or six miles and then turns to dirt. However, it is practical for passenger cars.) From San Luis Obispo, start at the intersection of Madonna and Los Osos Valley Roads in the Laguna Lake area, go northwest on Los Osos Valley Road to Prefumo Canyon Road (about .75 miles) and turn left. Then follow this country road through the beautiful Irish Hills to the same summit.

Vistas

If you prefer to keep your feet—and your car—on level ground while taking in the view, the following locations offer excellent down-to-earth views and photographic opportunities. (Note: *A Drive through History* on pages 75-106 details other good vantage points.)

4. Laguna Lake Park—From Highway 101, follow Madonna Road southwest to the park entrance and turn right. At the first opportunity, turn left, pass the children's playground area and turn right. Follow this road to the parking area near the boat launch. The view from here is good—you get a close-up look at San Luis Mountain and can follow the line of *morros* to the summit of Hollister Peak in the distance—but, if you're willing to take a short walk, it gets better. Just follow the flat, well-maintained exercise trail to the north end of the park. At its end, San Luis Mountain is directly on the right, followed by Bishop and Chumash Peaks and Cerro Romualdo. In the distance you'll see the craggy summit of Hollister Peak.

Bishop Peak (center) and Chumash Peak with Laguna Lake in the foreground.

5. O'Connor Way—From the Laguna Lake area of San Luis Obispo, head northwest on Los Osos Valley Road, turn right on Foothill Boulevard, then left on O'Connor Way. As you make the turn, San Luis Mountain is on your immediate right (across Foothill Boulevard). O'Connor Way winds past Bishop Peak, Chumash Peak and Cerro Romualdo on its way into the Cuesta College campus. Once past Cerro Romualdo, you can either turn around and backtrack or drive through the campus to Highway 1 and turn right (south) to return to San Luis Obispo or left (north) to go to Morro Bay.

Morro Rock framed by giant boulders at the summit of Prefumo Canyon and See Canyon Roads.

The view of Cerro Cabrillo from the Elfin Forest trailhead.

---

6. Elfin Forest Trailhead—From the intersection of Los Osos Valley Road and South Bay Boulevard in the Los Osos/Baywood Park area, take South Bay Boulevard north to Santa Ysabel Avenue and turn left, then right on 16th Street. Park at the end of the road and follow one of the many trails which lead into the Morro Estuary Natural Preserve (aka El Moro Elfin Forest). Thanks to the efforts of the members of Small Wilderness Area Preservation (SWAP), this 51-acre parcel of dunes, marshes and pygmy oaks is the newest addition to Morro Bay State Park. It's a beautiful refuge and definitely worth a visit. But, you don't have to go into the preserve to get a good look at the *morros*. Just walk a short distance up the trail to the first rise. From here the view of Morro Rock, Black Hill, Cerro Cabrillo, No Name Hill and Hollister Peak is breathtaking with the point of Cerro Romualdo and the crown of Bishop Peak visible in the distance.

Afterword

he *morros* figure prominently in my life. From my study at home, I look out upon the tawny slopes of Bishop Peak. At the office, the silhouette of two peaks decorates each piece of San Luis Obispo County Land Conservancy stationery.

These mountains lie at the very heart of San Luis Obispo County. They give us shelter from the perennial wind, constant visual contact with nature, a "sense of place" and a daily reminder that we still live close to the land.

Recently, I led a group of Sierra Club members to the top of Cerro San Luis Obispo (San Luis Mountain). As we watched the lingering sunset followed by the rise of a full moon, we looked out over the valleys that intersect below and were witness to the reasons why all of us should be concerned for the future of the *morros*. A pall of yellow haze was trapped by a typical spring inversion layer over Price Canyon to the south, probably generated by the diesel emissions from oil wells. Pacific Gas and Electric Company power lines snaked their way over the Los Osos Valley. And as the lights came on in the neighborhoods below, they illuminated the assault of the growing city against its embracing peaks and hillsides.

What will it truly mean to try to "save the peaks?" It is axiomatic for most conservationists interested in "saving" anything to call for public acquisition of the resource, followed, in most cases, by development of managed trails and other recreational uses. In the case of the Nine Sisters, however, we must look for a unique solution for the peaks are too important a resource to risk a bruising (and ultimately, losing) battle.

What is the ultimate goal? The first step should should not be to acquire the peaks as a "linear State Park," but to *manage* them as a National Natural Landmark. This can be initiated by a unilateral action of the Secretary of the Interior and would not require any disturbance of the existing mix of public and private ownership. Eventually, scenic easements should be acquired or dedicated on the most visible slopes (particularly along Highway 1) and free title should be secured to the top of Bishop Peak, taking advantage of the 1983 dedication to the California State Park Foundation. And limited public access should certainly be considered for Bishop Peak.

On the whole, however, the *morros* can continue to be a fundamental part of the "picture postcard" landscape of San Luis Obispo County without resorting to a heavy-handed conservation campaign. Most of the existing landowners—many of them third- and fourth- generation descendants of the original land grantees—are good stewards of the peaks. We should take whatever time is necessary to work with them in resolving the future of the peaks. But we should not hesitate to start down the road....

—*John Ashbaugh*
Executive Director
San Luis Obispo County Land Conservancy

Selected Glossary

Every effort was made to avoid an abundance of technical terms in this book, but a few were necessary in order to ensure accuracy and some slipped in as part of quotations. Although most of these are explained in the text, it is hoped that that the following list of terms and definitions will aid the reader in his understanding of the geology fundamental to the formation and appreciation of the *morros*.

Andesite (an´-de-site)—A dark colored volcanic rock consisting mainly of plagioclase feldspar and one or more mafic (rich in dark ferromagnesium) minerals such as biotite, hornblende or pyroxene.

Asthenosphere (as-then´-o-sphere)—The dense, plastic layer of the earth's mantle which is below the lithosphere, estimated to be about 150 miles thick. The nine tectonic plates ride on this layer.

Dacite (day´-site)—A fine-grained volcanic rock with the same general composition as andesite, but having more alkalic (sodium and potassium) and less calcic (lime or calcium) feldspar and usually more quartz.

Granophyre (gran´-o-phyre)—A porphyritic rock of granitic composition characterized by a crystalline-granular groundmass.

Intrusive rock (in-tru´-sive)—Rock that has, in a molten state, forced its way into pre-existing rock.

Igneous (ig´-ne-ous)—Said of a rock that has solidified from molten or partly molten state. One of the three classes of rock, the other two being metamorphic and sedimentary.

Lithosphere (lith´-o-sphere)—The crust and upper mantle of the earth comprised of the nine tectonic plates.

Magma (mag´-ma)—Naturally occurring molten rock generated within the earth from which igneous rocks have solidified.

Miocene (Mi´-o-cene)—An epoch of the early Tertiary period, 25 to 10 million years ago when grazing mammals were widespread. The term comes from *mio* meaning "less "and *cene* meaning "recent." It is generally believed that the *morros* formed during this tiime.

Oligocene (Ol´-i-go-cene)—An epoch of the early Tertiary period, 40 to 25 million years ago. The term comes from the Greek *oligo*, meaning "few" or "little" and *cene*, meaning "recent." It preceded the Miocene epoch.

Petrography (pe-trog´-ra-phy)—The branch of geology dealing with the description and systematic classification of rocks, especially by means of microscopic examination.

Phenocrysts (phe´-no-cryst)—Any of the conspicuous crystals in a porphyritic igneous rock.

Plate tectonics—A theory of global tectonics in which the lithosphere is divided into a number of crustal plates, each of which moves on the plastic asthenophere more or less independently to collide with, slide under or move past adjacent plates. The collision of the Pacific and North American plates during the Miocene epoch is fundamental to the geology of California as a whole and the *morros* in particular.

Plagioclase (pla´-gi-o-clase)—A group of feldspar minerals carrying the general chemical formula of sodium, calcium, aluminum silicate. Feldspars are the most widespread of any mineral group and constitute 60 percent of the earth's crust.

Pliocene (Pli´-o-cene)—An epoch of the Tertiary period, 10 to 2 million years ago. The term comes from *plio* or *pleo*, meaning "more" and *cene* meaning "recent." It succeeded the Miocene epoch and was characterized by the uplifting of mountains, the increase in size and number of mammals and global cooling.

Plug—A vertical pipelike body of cooled magma that represents a former volcanic vent, especially if standing as an erosional remnant.

Porphyry (por´-phy-ry)—Any igneous rock containing conspicuous phenocrysts in a fine-grained groundmass; a porphyritic igneous rock.

Pseudomorph (pseu´-do-morph)—A mineral having the outward appearance of another mineral that it has replaced by chemical action.

Salinian Block—The part of the earth's crust (and California in particular) which is west of the San Andreas Fault and is moving northwestward with the Pacific plate.

Siliceous (si-li´-ceous)—Said of a rock or other substance containing abundant silica.

Spreading ridges (aka mid-oceanic ridge)—Continuous massive underwater mountain ranges of rugged topography extending through the North and South Atlantic Oceans, the Indian Ocean and the South Pacific Ocean. The peaks range from about one-half to nearly two miles high and are about 900 miles wide. The chain is over 52,000 miles long. According to the theory of Plate Tectonics, new sea floor is generated at these ridges. (Example: East Pacific Rise.)

Subduction (sub-duc´-tion)—In the theory of plate tectonics, the process by which collision of crustal plates results in one plate being drawn down or overridden by another, localized along the juncture (**subduction zone**) of two plates. It is believed that the *morros* were the result of widespread volcanic activity following the subduction of the Farallon plate and East Pacific Rise by the North American plate about 25 million years ago.

Tertiary (Ter´-ti-ar-y)—The first period of the Cenozoic era, covering the span of time between 65 million and 2 million years ago. It is divided into five epochs—the Paleocene, Eocene, Oligocene, Miocene and Pliocene—and is characterized by the development and proliferation of mammals.

Additional Reading

The following is not meant to be a complete listing of references used in researching this text. Instead, it includes classic sources which specifically mention the *morros*—either in a geologic or historic sense and a few recommended geologic texts. It is intended as an aid to the lay reader who has an interest in studying the original historic material and learning more about California geology. Professional papers which deal in-depth with the petrography of the *morros* are not included, but some are available to the serious scholar at the California Polytechnic State University library and at the Morro Bay State Park Museum of Natural History library.

Classic References

Angel, Myron, *History of San Luis Obispo County (1883).* Valley Publishers, Fresno, California, 1979.

Brewer, William H., *Up and Down California in 1860-1864.* University of California Press, Berkeley, California, 1949.

California State Mining Bureau, *Thirteenth Report of the State Mineralogist,* California State Printing Office, Sacramento, California, 1896.

California State Mining Bureau, *The Structural and Industrial Materials of California, Bulletin 38.* California State Printing Office, Sacramento, California, 1906.

California State Mining Bureau, *Mines and Mineral Resources of the Counties of Monterey, San Benito, San Luis Obispo, Santa Barbara, Ventura.* California State Printing Office, Sacramento, California, 1917.

California State Mining Bureau, *Report XV of the State Mineralogist; Mines and Mineral Resources of Portions of California.* California State Printing Office, Sacramento, California, 1919.

Crespí, Father Juan, *Captain Portolá in San Luis Obispo County in 1769.* Tabula Rasa Press, Morro Bay, California, 1984.

Diller, J.S. and others, *Guidebook of the Western United States, Part D.—The Shasta Route and Coastline.* United States Geologic Survey, Government Printing Office, Washington, D.C., 1916.

Fairbanks, H.W., *Description of the San Luis Quadrangle, California: Geologic Atlas, San Luis Folio 101,* United States Geological Survey, 1904.

Jennings, C.W., *Geologic Map of California, San Luis Obispo Sheet* (scale 1:250,000). California Division of Mines and Geology, 1958,

San Luis Obispo County Planning Department, *A Specific Plan for Preservation of the Morros*, 1972.

Strong, F. and Associates, *A Specific Plan for the Morros*, 1973.

Geology Texts

Bates, Robert L. and Jackson, Julia A, *Dictionary of Geological Terms (Third Edition)*, Anchor Books, Doubleday, New York, 1984.

Chipping, David H., *The Geology of San Luis Obispo County*, California Polytechnic State University, 1987.

Hill, Mary, *California Landscape: Origin and Evolution*, University of California Press, Berkeley, California, 1984.

Howard, Arthur D., *Geologic History of Middle California.* University of California Press, Berkeley, California, 1979.

Iocopi, Robert, *Earthquake Country: How, Why and Where Earthquakes Strike in California.* Lane Publishing Company, Menlo Park, California, 1971.

Lambert, David and the Diagram Group, *The Field Guide to Geology.* Facts On File, New York, 1988.

Norris, Robert M. and Webb, Robert W., *Geology of California.* John Wiley & Sons, Inc., New York, 1976.

Sharp, Robert P., *Geology Field Guide to Coastal Southern California.* Kendall/Hunt Publishing Company, Dubuque, Iowa, 1978.

Sharp, Robert P., *Geology Field Guide to Southern California.* Kendall/Hunt Publishing Company, Dubuque, Iowa, 1972.

Index

Photographer's Notes

All photographs in this book (with the exception of the historic images) were shot with either a Toyo 45A field camera or a Canon T-90 35mm SLR. Although lenses ranged from 90mm to 300mm for the 4x5 equipment and from 24mm to 600 mm for the 35mm cameras, I found the longer lenses (100 or 200mm for 35mm and 210 or 300mm for 4x5) made more visual sense because they allowed me to isolate the subject matter.

I shot exclusively with Kodak T-Max 100 and 400 (35mm and 4x5 sizes) or Agfa Pan APX 25 (35mm only) films and processed in either Agfa Rodinol or Edwal Fg7 developers. The original prints were made on Ilford Multigrade FB paper processed in Dektol and Selenium toned.

All shooting locations were chosen because they are readily accessible. Most are right off of the road and can be easily found on the driving tour. I hiked several of the peaks and heartily recommend the hike to the top of Black Hill where the photographer is rewarded with wonderful views of the coast, surrounding valleys and adjacent hills.

Early morning or late afternoon light is ideal for bringing out the textures of the rocky crags of the *morros*, but photographers should be advised that morning fog and afternoon wind must often be contended with.

In photographing for this and previous books, I have rediscovered the beauty of the Central Coast. I hope that you, too, will discover the charm and enchantment of this last vestige of "Old California."

—*Joseph A. Dickerson*

Other Titles From EZ Nature Books

History of San Luis Obispo County, 1883, Myron Angel. Hard cover, reprint, $37.50

California's Chumash Indians, Santa Barbara Museum of Natural History, $5.95

Santa Barbara Companion, Tom Tuttle. A guidebook. $8.95

Ventura County Companion, Tom Tuttle. A guide book. $8.95

Bicycling San Luis Obispo County, Sharon Lewis Dickerson. A guidebook. $6.95

California Indian Watercraft, Richard Cunningham. Water transport from pre-mission days to the mid-19th century. $12.95

The Life and Times of Fray Junipero Serra, Msgr. Francis J. Weber. Extractions from Rev. Maynard Geiger's immense work. Revised reprint. $5.95

Hearst's Dream, Taylor Coffman. How the Hearst Castle came to be. $8.95

Sentinels of Solitude, Ehlers and Gibbs. Color photographs of lighthouses of the United States west coast. Revised reprint. $14.95

Making the Most of San Luis Obispo County, Sharon Lewis Dickerson. A guidebook. $9.95

Old Mission San Luis Obispo de Tolosa, Kathleen Anderson. A miniature cut-out-and-color model. $3.95

San Luis Obispo: A Look Back Into the Middle Kingdom, Dan Krieger. Revised reprint, $17.95

Mountain Biking the Central Coast, Carol Berlund. A guidebook. $7.95

Order from: EZ Nature Books, P.O. Box 4206, San Luis Obispo, CA 93403. For shipping, add $1.00 for the first book and $.50 for each additional. California residents add 6.25% sales tax.

2847